SURVIVAL

OF THE

YAVAPAI

By Frieda Ann Eswonia

Published by Sedona Heritage Publishing, held by the Sedona Historical Society, Inc.

Visit Our Website

 www.sedonamuseum.org

Like us on Facebook

Facebook.com/sedonamuseum

View Our Calendar of Events

 Sedonamuseum.org/calendar

Printed in the United States of America

Cover art by CW Schoonover

ISBN: 978-0692454046

FRIEDA ANN ESWONIA

Mother of three boys and one girl; called "Grandma" by most of her family and friends; a teacher of the language and history of the Yavapai Tribe of American Indians, whose ancestral home and legendary beginning is from the Verde Valley of central Arizona.

Frieda has worked in and with Tribal and State Courts as an advocate with the Indian Child Welfare Act and is active in Tribal, Local, State and Federal Government. She resides on the Clarkdale Reservation of the Yavapai-Apache Nation.

Dedication

This book is dedicated to my Lord and Savior, "Jesus The Messiah", who has been with me all my life— protecting, guiding and directing me.

And especially to my paternal grandmother, Jun Tha La Charley, who raised me in the Clarkdale Indian Community, after my mother's death. Her undying love and care for all of her son, Samuel Russell's eleven children, are special memories that none of us could ever forget. I learned so much from my father's mother who willingly accepted the responsibility of not only caring for her son's children, but teaching us what she knew about Yavapai history, legends and mostly the Yavapai language. She was always happy to give of herself to help us children all that she could and because of that, I know about the Yavapai People, most of which came to me from her.

Also, to the encouragement from my siblings, especially my beloved brother, Daniel B. Russell, who has gone on to the "Happy Hunting Ground" and to my beloved sister, Winona Durant, the two who were always there with encouragement.

And to my immediate family: husband, Dale Gohr, three sons, LeRoy, Jr. , Sammy, Eugene and to my daughter, Sherrilee, and granddaughter, Alexia. You have all been my greatest joy and comfort throughout my life.

TOGETHER—BUT YEARS APART

**My Paternal Grandmother – Nya Moda
<u>Jun Tha la Charley</u>**

Winona and Dave

At Newport Beach when we were in the
Los Angeles area for; "Doe's Wedding".

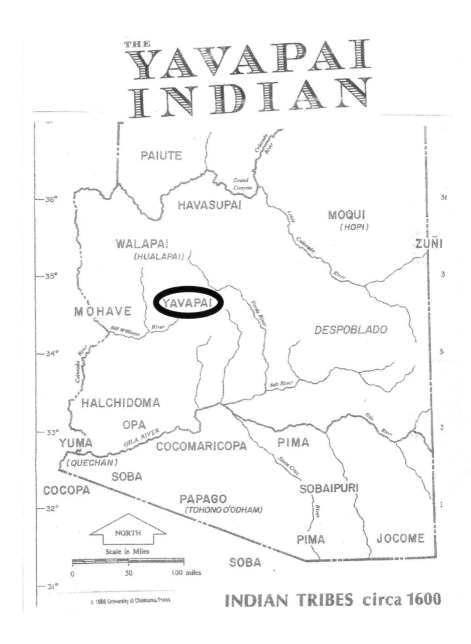

THE YAVAPAI INDIAN

PAIUTE

Colorado River

Grand Canyon

36°

HAVASUPAI

MOQUI
(HOPI)

ZUÑI

WALAPAI
(HUALAPAI)

Little Colorado River

35°

MOHAVE

YAVAPAI

Bill Williams River

Verde River

DESPOBLADO

34°

Colorado River

Salt River

HALCHIDOMA

OPA

GILA RIVER

Gila River

33°

YUMA
(QUECHAN)

COCOMARICOPA

PIMA

Santa Cruz

SOBA

COCOPA

PAPAGO
(TOHONO O'ODHAM)

SOBAIPURI

32°

River

NORTH

PIMA

JOCOME

Scale in Miles

0   50   100 miles

SOBA

31°

© 1988 University of Oklahoma Press

INDIAN TRIBES circa 1600

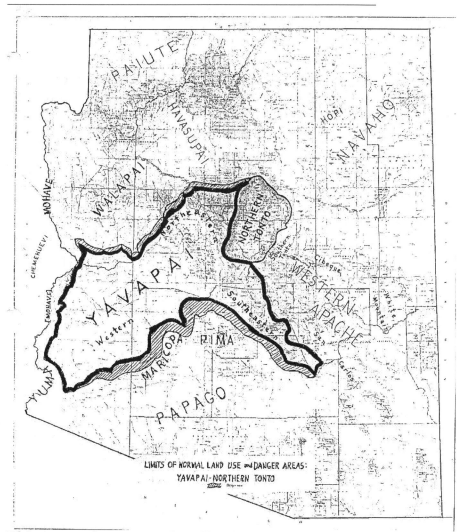

This map shows graphically the ranging areas of the various tribes during the early contact with Europeans. This shows the Navajo and Apache and probably comes from the early 1800's although I cannot be absolutely sure of its origin or authenticity.

Frieda

Author's note:

Anytime I use the words "**American Indian**" it is in reference to the "**Indigenous People of the Americas.**" For lack of a better way to distinguish my Ancestry from that of the people from the country of "India" and the "East Indies" both terms ("American Indian" and "Native-American") are used in my writing and speaking.

CHAPTER 1
A TRIBES STRUGGLE TO SURVIVE A LOST IDENTITY

In the beginning, the Indian people of this country had been hurt by many broken promises made by the United States Government. There were many broken treaties--our land, culture and language was taken from us; yet, the Indian people survived. This story is of my people, the Yavapai and our survival. There was a movie made years ago with an actor by the name of, Jeff Chandler, and you might possibly remember the particular movie he starred in as a great Indian Chief named "Cochise". He dramatically stated in that movie called "Broken Arrow", "I break the Arrow"-- signifying that there were to be no more wars with the U.S. Government. Chief Cochise was instrumental in bringing an end to the Indian wars in central Arizona and thus was responsible for deterring the genocide of my Native American people. Who were these people that I am talking about that were almost wiped off the face of this earth by genocide?

Well, one of these groups of people that I have ties to is called the Yavapai-Apache Nation. It is made up of two tribes – the Yavapai and the Apache. I, myself, am a full-blood Yavapai Indian and I grew up living with my grandmother and attending elementary public school in Clarkdale, Arizona (K – 2nd grades) then moving to Prescott, Arizona to live with my father (and attending public school there- 3-12th grade) where I graduated from high school in 1957. My mother had passed away early in life and I had been sent to live with my grandmother in Clarkdale, Arizona before going to live with my father in Prescott, Arizona.

While living in the Clarkdale Indian Community with my paternal grandmother or "Moda" as she would be referred to in the Yavapai language, my first language was 'Yavapai". My Moda never learned the English Language and only spoke Yavapai. This was true also of most of the tribal members during that time as they had not yet learned to speak English nor did they really want to learn the English language. That was during the years of 1938 – 1946. I consider it a blessing to have learned my native language and culture at a young age and to have kept and used it all my life; because it has helped me retain my identity. I know who I am and I know about my heritage. This is all so very important!

I tell my people that, "We, as Indian People, need to remember the past; but we also need to look to the future. We can have pride in our ancestors if we take time to learn about them. I know that I am proud and have always been proud of who I am, even though, I spent most of my adult life off of the reservation.

However, the pride that I have in being an Indian does not seem to be the case with many of the other

Indians that did grow up on the different reservations around the country. It seems to me that most of them feel that they are **"Just another Indian"**. While living in Albuquerque, New Mexico, I attended the Assembly of God Church where, Pastor William Fragua, who is from the Jemez Pueblo, did not like to hear anyone say that they were, **"Just another Indian"** phrase at all. He would often tell the congregation that **"No**, we are not "Just another Indian"; but we are **somebody** and, "**a somebody**", who should be proud of who we are.

How then, can we, the Indian people, have pride in our heritage? Herein, follows the story of my people, the Yavapai Indians, and our struggles to move forward and try to "fit in" with this modern society. **What is it that we must learn** about our ancestors and their legacy, in particular, so we can move forward with pride and know that we are not, **"Just another Indian!"**

The Yavapai Tribe is a small tribe. We do not have a large land base; because most had been taken away by the Federal Government. Our land base is very small and segmented; and too, we share our Indian Nation with an Apache Tribe. The Federal Government set both tribes on the same land base—two tribes from a very different culture, language and heritage.

As it was from the beginning, the Federal Government always thought that all Indians were the same. The Yavapai were known to associate a lot with the Apaches; but that did not mean that we were the same -- physically or culturally The Yavapai belong to the Hokan Language Family which is composed of Upland Yuman composed of the "Pai Groups" the Hualapai, Havasupai, and Yavapai. There is also the Up River Yuman, Delta River Yuman, Southern and Baja California, Yuman plus 14 other Hokan Language Family Groups.

The Verde Valley, where the Yavapai are from, is an area which is known to have once been a great geological legacy. Today, it is only known as a high desert area. However, because of the legacy, fossil traces of fish have been found among the red rocks in the Sedona Area. Another fact is that tracks of giant creatures have been found. This shows the life that was in the Verde Valley before the great ice ages; and too, archeologists have found huge tusks and jaws of a giant mammoth in this area, which was unearthed at the Cement Plant in Clarkdale, discovered in1981 (and, this area is near the Clarkdale Indian Community, where I now live. So, this is a very interesting area from which the Yavapai originated!

However, in order to learn more about the Yavapai from this area, you first have to know our "Origin Story". I will now go into that "Yavapai Origin Story", -- of which there are several versions.

Frieda Ann Eswonia

The Yavapai, as was told to me by my Moda, emerged from the underworld, after a great flood at

HOKAN LANGUAGE FAMILY

HOKAN LANGUAGES

> Upland Yuman:
>
>> Hualapai,
>>
>> Havasupai,
>>
>> Yavapai
>
> Up River Yuman:
>
>> Mohave, Yuma (Quechan)
>
> Delta River Yuman:
>
>> Cocopah, Kohuana, Halyikwamai
>
> Southern and Baja California, Yuman:
>
>> Diegueno, Kamia, Akwa'ala, Kiliwa, Nyakipa
>
> Seri Language
>
> Pomo Family
>
> Shastan, Yanan, and Palaihnihan Families
>
> Washo Language
>
> Salinan, Chumashan, and Baselen Families
>
> Comecrudan Family
>
> Coahuiltecan Language
>
> Tlapanecan Family
>
> Tequistlatecan Family
>
> Jicaque Language

These are Languages that are related to my own Yavapai Language and some of these are considerably different; enough so, that we do not readily understand each other. However, in the "Movies" it would appear as though one man would be able to "Talk Indian" and interpret for all: Artistic Privilege; Right? ☺.

a spot that is now known to many now as "Montezuma Well". Here is how the story goes.......

YAVAPAI CREATION STORY

Many years ago, the Yavapai lived in this land until there came a time when there was a great drought and nothing would grow for the people to eat. The Yavapai People fearing that they would all die in this famine, sent a humming bird ("Mina Mina)" as he is called in Yavapai, to seek a new place where the Yavapai could go and live. (At that time, of course, was when all the animals could talk to each other and to humans also.) The Yavapai then said to the "Mina Mina" that wherever he could find good, fertile land and a place where the Yavapai might thrive is where the people would go. The "Mina Mina" flew around and found a great tree that grew on up through a hole in the sky into an "Upper world". The "Mina Mina" then flew into the hole in the sky and came to a place where there was fertile ground and where plants were growing. It was a good land! Therefore, when the "Mina Mina" found all this, he flew back and told the people that he had found a beautiful place in the Upper world where the

Yavapai might live. The "Mina Mina" said, "Let's go up there". So the people and the animals went up into the new world by climbing on the great tree that the "Mina Mina" had shown them. The people and animals climbed without stopping until they came out through the hole in the sky to the new world. They did, however, leave behind the frog folks in the "Under world". The people forgot about the frog folks being left behind and lived happily in this new land for a long time. Until one day, the flooding happened again. The people saw water coming from the hole that led to the underworld and they knew they would all drown from the water which was quickly flooding the ground. They knew that this flood was being made by the frog folks whom they had left behind in the Underworld. Knowing also that they would all drown, they had to act quickly. They hollowed out a log and put food, water and a young maiden inside. This maiden drifted through the flood waters and survived the flood. She later landed at a high place in the Sedona Area when the flood waters subsided near, what is now called "Boynton Canyon". This woman lived for many years in this area and is known by our people as "First Woman". This story goes on with First Woman, later becoming intimate with the Sun and then having a daughter whom she called "Kamalapukwia".

When this daughter became older, she also went to the Sun, who knowing her as his daughter, sent her to another Heavenly Being," The Cloud" for whom she bore a son. Her son was then called, 'Skatagaomja". As she aged, First Woman became known as "Gumwedma Buque" in Yavapai (which fittingly means "Old Woman").   And so, the Yavapai survived the great flood and continued to propagate and grow in numbers in this area now called the Verde Valley.

Because of this legend, the Verde River Valley is the area where the Yavapai lived then and still live today. There are four tribal bands of the Yavapai Indians: There is the "Yavbe" or Yavapai from the Prescott Area, "Wipukpaya" which means "people at the base of the mountain" or the Sedona area and present day, Clarkdale and Camp Verde areas, "Gwevkopaya", means "southern people", referring to the Fort McDowell area and "Tolkapaya", those that live in the middle such as Peeples Valley/Chino Valley or Skull Valley within a fifty mile radius of Prescott. My Father was from the Wiipukapaya (this is the ancestral band of my father), Samuel Adams Russell). My mother's band of Yavapai were "Gwevkopaya" and were from the Ft. McDowell area.

These early Yavapai lived, farmed, hunted and gathered food in a lifestyle that continued without any real disruption in an area of over 10 million acres in central and western Arizona until the 1850s invasion of the settlers and miners into northern Arizona. In 1863, gold was discovered and the area became filled with prospectors and miners who disrupted the Indian lifestyle. Because their lifestyle was disrupted, the Yavapai became a group of starving Indians. The settlers had invaded their gathering and farming locations and then they generally chose to camp near water and would often kill any Indian that tried to get water. This made the Indians and the settlers highly incompatible. On the other hand, the Apache were already fighting back by making raids on the settlers—killing them and stealing horses to use in combat. However, more and more often, the Yavapai were being blamed for the attacks of the Apaches on the settlers and were killed along with the Apache.

CHAPTER 2
YAVAPAI AND APACHE

Let me explain a little more about the Apaches. They were and are a different ethnic origin from the Yavapai. The Apache speak a language belonging to the Athabaskan stock, totally unrelated to the Hokan-Yuman language, which is spoken by the Yavapai. Although some intermarriage occurred early on, the Yavapai and Apache remained separate and distinct from each other. Each tribe claimed the use of separate hunting and gathering areas. It was generally understood that the Mazatlan Mountains were the boundary between the Yavapai and Apache. Although the two tribes, Yavapai and Apache are not alike, it was the Federal Government who generally claimed that "All Indians" were the same and put these two tribes on the same reservation to live together.

YAVAPAI COUNTY

So it was that the Yavapai and Apache Tribes were put on the same reservation by the Federal government . The Federal Government did not consider that the Yavapai were the original Indians of this area and that the Apache were new comers — arriving after the 1860's. "Yavapai County" was the name given to the area, named after my people, the Yavapai, who claimed it as their home land. This land extended from the Verde and Salt Rivers to the mouth of the Bill Williams River on the Colorado. Arizona was originally made up of four counties and the largest was where the first territorial capital was located in Prescott, Arizona. All the other tribes in Arizona have legends about migrating into their territory from somewhere else, but the Yavapai do not. The Apaches arrived in central Arizona sometime after A.D. 1600 according to maps of the area at that time; and the Apaches do remember a time when they used to live further to the north. That is one of the main differences between the Yavapai and Apache and that is that the Yavapai do not remember a time when they came here from somewhere else.

Even in this Yavapai land area, the early Spanish explorers noted the separation of the different bands of Yavapai. The Yavapai bands today live in three different communities, the Yavapai/Apache Nation in the Verde Valley, the Fort McDowell Yavapai Nation located near Fountain Hills and the Prescott Yavapai Nation located in Prescott, Arizona.

According to written history, it was on April 30, 1583, when Spanish explorer, Antonio Espejo and Father Bernaldino Beltran made their first contact with the Yavapai Indians. This first contact was in the region between Flagstaff and the point where they descended into the Verde Valley. Here, they found the first Yavapai settlement. The Spanish explorers then followed the Yavapai guides up to the Verde mines near present-day Jerome, Arizona. The Spanish then wrote:

"The region is inhabited by mountainous people". The explorers then described the "mountainous people" and said that they had "crowns of painted sticks" on their heads and that these people gave them metals as a sign of peace. The Spanish also said that these people were peaceful.

Throughout the rest of the Spanish period up to 1821, there were no known explorations into Yavapai Territory. Even 150 years after these earliest explorations into Yavapai territory, the Spaniards did not have any known contact with the Yavapai in the area. However, historians have said that some of the Indians whom they called "Apache" were in fact, Yavapai. Most of the time, it did not matter to "Whites" whether the Indians were one tribe or another, they were usually all grouped together and called "Apache".

The American entrance into the Yavapai area began a little after 1860. Exploring and trapping parties had come into the area occasionally, but as late as 1860, neither the Mexicans nor the Americans had made any effort to settle there. However, in later 1862 and early 1863, Captain Walker and Pauline Weaver led parties of miners into the Yavapai area. Mining camps were established in the region of Prescott and along the Hassayampa River "Aha se yaama" which is a Yavapai word meaning "where the water flows". These camps stimulated exploration and settlement into Yavapai Territory which soon went as far north as Chino Valley, as far east as Agua Fria, and as far west as La Paz. United States troops then set up Camp Whipple close to

Prescott in1863. The following year, Prescott became the capital of Arizona Territory and Camp Whipple, the U.S, Army Headquarters for the Department of Arizona. Other settlements were made, -- Wickenburg southwest of Prescott, Walnut Grove on the Hassayampa, and the settlement of Clear Creek in 1864, on the Verde River. The United States Army then set up additional camps at Date Creek in1864, on the Verde River the same year, and at Ft. McDowell just north of the Salt River in1865. By 1867, ranches and mines were scattered along the Agua Fria and Hassayampa Rivers, and Big Bug Creek, Turkey Creek, and Kirkland Creek, and in the nearby valleys and mountains.

Thus, the Indian hostilities began with the arrival of the miners and people who were taking over the land area to stay. Conflicts began and continued until the round-up of the Indians by General Crook at Camp Verde.

ARIZONA FORTS & CAMPS OF THE FRONTIER ARMY

Sgt. F. ESERTON (Ret.)-CARTOGRAPHER
Col. ROBERT YOUNT, C.A.M.P. CONSULTANT

ECEMBER 3, 1972

The Army Forts and Camps in some cases became "Towns" sometimes taking the Fort Name sometimes changing the Name. This is logical because the Army settled near Good Water and Defendable Terrain; good places for Settlements..

CHAPTER 3
TURMOIL

When the Indians started to raid the settlements for food and water which was being taken away from them, the settlers also started fighting back and took their complaints to the United States Government. The U.S. Army came in and set up military forts to assist the settlers against the so-called "savages"; the major forts being at Camp Verde, Ft. Whipple, and Ft. McDowell. When even more and more settlers began to enter into Yavapai lands, it became even more troublesome for the Yavapai. They were often mistaken for Apaches, who made frequent raids on the settlers; the Yavapai were often killed in retaliation for the Apache attacks. The Army established forts in a lot of areas and a "round-up" of Indians began to "protect" the settlers who were taking up the Indian lands. This is when the Yavapai word for "people" worked against the Yavapai; because the Yavapai word for people "Abaja" sounded a lot like "Apache" to the soldiers who were out to kill Apaches. Whenever the Yavapai were asked who they were by the cavalry, they would answer "Abaja" which meant "people"; but it sounded like "Apache" to the soldiers so the Yavapai were often killed by the cavalry who thought they were Apaches.

In the year 1871, General George Crook had arrived in Arizona to command the fighting troops and fighting between the settlers and Indians. Under

Crook's command, in the years between 1871 and 1874, many Yavapai were taken to the Rio Verde Reservation. The concentration of the Yavapai Indians on the Rio Verde Reservation May 1, 1873, marks the date when, the United States took lands away from the Yavapai Indians, who originally used these lands not making any payment or compensation of the lands to the Indians.

In the fall of 1874, living on the Rio Verde Reservation, the Yavapai and Apache population was reduced by 1/3 as the people were unfamiliar with the rations they were given by the soldiers. They did not know how to cook the food that they were not used to eating so that many of the people died of hunger. It is said that they actually thought the soldiers were trying to poison them with these unknown food supplies. This practice of giving the Indians poisoned food had previously been done to get rid of the Indians and the Indians were very leery of accepting the food that the soldiers gave them.

It was not long though before the Rio Verde Reservation was closed in 1875, due to the infamous "Concentration Policy" which was an Order by the Federal Government by which all reservations were to be closed down and the Indians rounded up and relocated to the San Carlos Reservation, in what is sometimes called, "The Trail of Tears". All the Indians were rounded up and taken to the San Carlos Reservation and incarcerated there for twenty-five (25) years before they were allowed to return to the

Verde Valley. When they did return home, they found that their lands had been taken by the settlers. The Indians settled on what was left of their land and tried to fit into this new culture which was totally unfamiliar to them! Almost all of the good land and water had been taken by settlers.

Here I will insert a story by Maggie Hayes (my paternal great aunt, (Jun Tha La Charley's sister), in her own words, regarding her life during this period. Maggie Hayes was taken back east when the Indian children were rounded up and taken to Indian Boarding Schools. Maggie was educated in those schools back east and could therefore communicate pretty well in English. Maggie, was not physically a lot like my grandmother Jun Tha La Charley, being much smaller in stature. Here is relayed the story of Maggie Hayes and her siblings births; and their lives during that period written in her own words.

The Maggie Hayes Story

"It is difficult to remember accurate details of my early childhood, but I will try. Because Indians kept no birth records, my birth date was established as May 16, 1885 arbitrarily, by the San Carlos Indian Agency. I was born at the original settlement of San Carlos Arizona Territory—the site that is now under the waters of the lake that was made with the building of Coolidge Dam.

My people were of the Yavapai Tribe. The translation of Yavapai into English is rather difficult, because "Pai" means "people", while "Yava" has a much deeper meaning that the word "mouth" signifies. It could also mean "law", "speak", "expressive", "silent", "spoken: The Yavapai's were noted for keeping their word, so we arrive at a reasonable meaning— "People Who Speak The Truth".

My mother had told me many stories of their homeland in the Verde Valley and of the time when the U.S. soldiers and Indian scouts rounded up many scattered bands of Indians— different tribes with different languages from a vast area, and brought them all together. They were to be transferred, against their wishes, to the San Carlos Indian Reservation. She estimated the number of Indians—men, women and children, to be around 3,000. They were herded like cattle, out of the Verde Valley towards the San Carlos Indian Reservation. Actually, less than half were able to survive the trip. (A reservation story shows that 1,400 arrived from Rio Verde Reservation).

This is the true story of the march to San Carlos as told to Maggie Hayes by her mother (Chudge ga hodva) or Mary Mitchell, which was the name given to her by the soldiers), in her mother's own words Maggie Hayes told this story of the March to San Carlos:

"We were many moons on the trip. We had to walk all the way. The soldiers had ponies to ride. There were no roads and very few trails. A lot of the Indians did not have moccasins; but those who did, gave them to others who needed them more. However even the moccasins wore out on the sharp rocks. Our clothing was torn to rags on the brush and cactus. With bleeding feet, weary in body, and sick at heart, many wanted to die. Many of the people did die. Rations were meager. It was winter time. At night we huddled together around the campfires to keep warm. Cold and hungry, we did our best to get a little rest. Many a loved one was left along the way either dead or dying--their bodies to be eaten by wild animals. We were not allowed to take the time nor did we have the strength to bury the dead.

The Middle three Adults left to right are: My Aunt; Daisy Russell, My Great Aunt: Maggie Hayes and her Daughter, My Cousin Fannie Hayes on the far left is; Clara Jackson and on the right is Vincent Randall's Mother, I do not recall her first name and I do not know the children's names.

These Ladies along with very few others, especially Nya Moda (My Grandmother) Tha la Charley; were the "Backbone of the Church in Clarkdale", and we were blessed to have them; even though I was too young to realize the value of these "Devout and Hardworking Ladies" at the time: I would like to Honor them here with a "Special Thank You" for the profound "Sense of Purpose" they helped instill in my thoughts and actions and have remained with me all of my life.

I wonder how much the effort of these Strong and Thoughtful Ladies helped form the overall character of others in the Yavapai-Apache Nation; today.

We waded across many streams. One river was running strong when we got to the crossing. We were forced to cross the best way we could. Some of the weaker ones were washed away down the river to a watery grave. Those of us who did survive the crossing were more like drowned rats than human beings. It was a pitiful sight, and we still had a long way to go— we would leave more dead and dying along the way."

Note: *Maggie said that the narrative was necessary to show how her parents and other members of the Yavapai Indian Tribe were brought to the San Carlos Indian Reservation along with Indians of other tribes. Maggie went on to say that it seemed to be the habit of historians and writers to refer to all Indians at San Carlos as being Apaches, but that it was not so. "The Apache, as well as their language, is as different from the Yavapai as is the Spanish and English from each other. Our temperaments, beliefs, the way of life, are also different from the Apache. So it was that all of the tribes were dumped on the San Carlos Indian Reservation together, unable to understand each other's languages and temperaments. They understood only vaguely, through interpreters, what was expected of them by their captors".*

Maggie continued: "This was the situation when my mother and father started a new life and were trying to raise a family. Their firstborn was a boy, born in about the year 1879. He died of smallpox. In about 1882, my sister Tha la was born. I was the third-born in the year 1885. They named me C-ah-hanna (meaning "Good Girl").

The fourth was a boy born in the year 1886. They named him Ne-pa-pai-ma (No Arrows). Then in 1889, my youngest brother was born. They called him Ka-thad-ah-hanna (Cunning, but Good). My father's name was Chudge Ka-hode-va (Up and Down Many Hills). In those days the Indians had no last names.

Life on the Reservation was not good. The weekly rations consisted of flour, sugar, coffee, salt and meat that was hardly sufficient for two days, let alone a week. Many of the Indians scoured the desert and the nearby mountains and hills for edible plants and seeds in order to supplement their food supply. There was a scant supply at its best for the people to eat; and there were so many searching and hungry mouths to feed.

Father was pressed into service as a scout. This service was compensated for in part when each year they would give him a pony or a sow. Also, his meals and clothing were furnished. As a scout, he was able to relocate in an area near Globe, Arizona, called Coyote Springs. We moved there about the year 1886, along with a few other Yavapai Indians. The foraging for wild food was more fruitful. Wild hay and firewood could be gathered and sold to residents of Globe for a little money with which to buy some food and clothing.

Things were getting better for us by the year 1890. We had our own little garden and some ponies. Then one night, in the early part of that year, they brought father home in an army hospital blanket, with a very high fever and at the point of death with tuberculosis. The rigors of the grueling trip from the Verde had taken more out of him than he would let us suspect. He had carried his secret alone for 13 years.

I can still remember many of the details. The Indian medicine man came to bring good medicine and to sing and dance for Yack-Ah-Pava, my father. He had been a great hunter with the bow and arrows in his homeland along the Verde River. So, the Great Spirit called Yack-Ah-Pava to the Happy Hunting Round just three days after he was brought home to his family at Coyote Springs Camp.

This was a sad time for all of us, in a lot more ways than just the loss of our father and protector. We were to learn how cruel the Indian could be with a defenseless widow. My father's own brother appropriated our livestock and anything he thought was of value, on the grounds that he was the heir to his brother's estate. So, rather than cause trouble by reporting the incident to the agency, mother let him get away with it.

Chudge-ka-hode-va, stripped of everything of value, was left with four small children to raise — the youngest still strapped to the familiar Indian cradleboard. There was nothing else to do but return to the reservation and her people. Sister Tha la and I went to live with our paternal grandmother and mother took Ne-pa-pai-ma and Ka-thod-ah-hanna to live with her relatives. The separation from mother was not severe since we lived in the vicinity of each, Me-eth-tho (Ghost), or grandmother, was kind and good to us.

We had not been back on the reservation quite two years when I was singled out as one of the younger children to be sent away to the Indian School at Grand Junction, Colorado. Some 40 or 50 children, ages about 6 to 10, were loaded into wagons one morning, and were started on the long wagon journey from San Carlos to Fort Bowie. There they were to be transferred to the Southern Pacific Railroad. I was on my way to an 11-year exile from my family.

About six months before this time, a group of the older children had been gathered up and sent to school, amid protests of their parents.

So when the younger ones were taken, the resistance and feeling ran high. Soldiers were on hand to maintain order and to keep the mothers from recovering their children. It was a sad parting; mothers and children were sobbing wildly.

I shall never forget how some of the mothers, including my own, followed the wagons, mile after mile, hoping that some of the children would escape. One of the mothers was very big and heavy and she had a hard time keeping up with the wagons. Mother and one other woman would help her by letting her hold onto each one of them. They must have finally become too exhausted to follow us any further than Ft. Thomas, for I never saw them after that.

Only the imagination could fill in the gap here and tell the story of the anguish that must have been theirs as they trudged those many, weary miles back to the reservation, broken-hearted and empty-handed. Why their babies had been taken away, they could not understand.

It was well that an older Indian accompanied us on the trip. He was able to calm us down and quiet our fears. His own daughter was along also so he reasoned with us that no father would allow his own little girl to go to a place that was not good for her. None of the children could speak a word of English so he was also our interpreter and saw to it that everyone was fed and our other needs were provided. His was no easy task as we must have been quite a handful. He also had to return to the reservation and report to the unhappy parents about their children and what a nice place they were now living in now. I suspect few believed him. It was a 1-day trip on the wagons and it seemed that the train trip took two days and two nights. Train service was much slower in those days.

When we finally arrived at Grand Junction, they stopped the train for us right across from the Indian School. We were all glad that the trip was over; but most of all, we were relieved when we saw some of the children who had been brought here some six months earlier. They were very much alive and apparently, very happy. I could hardly believe my ears when I heard them talking English and wondered at the time if it was at all possible that I might be able to do the same thing. That problem ceased to worry me for long since the methods they used at the school were very effective. Soon we had been there long enough to get acquainted with the fundamentals of English. Then when we were caught conversing in the Indian tongue, we were put on a bread and water diet and our play activities and social periods were suspended for a time. This got old after a couple of treatments and English became no problem at all.

School took on a completely different aspect and was far from being the terrible place that I had envisioned it to be. In fact, it was the nicest place I had ever been in my life. We were treated firmly but with kindness, and I can't remember ever getting really homesick. Maybe one of the reasons was that I had been somewhat weaned away from my mother while staying with my grandmother.

The girl's dormitory where I was assigned sleeping quarters had about 20 beds. Two girls slept in a bed. It was the first bed I ever slept in since I had always before slept on the ground. My roommate was an Apache girl by the name of Emma, which was given to her at the school. The name they assigned to me was Maggie Mitchell.

From the start of my schooling at Grand Junction, my favorite girlfriend was a Yavapai girl by; the name of Tu-ve-uiga (All mixed up), which they changed to Polly. She was always so happy and loved to sing. She had a beautiful singing voice and was always one of the leaders in our get-together songfests. We palled around together, even though she was three years my senior. It seems that I can still hear her singing at her work, which was cleaning and scrubbing the halls and the dormitories with some of the other girls. Polly left for the reservation the same year that Emma departed. I never saw them again.

School routine fell into somewhat of a fixed pattern: Lights out at 9:00, up bright and early in the morning, make our beds, get ready for breakfast, do our assigned tasks, and attend our classes.

Naturally we had to be disciplined occasionally, as all children do, for getting involved in mischievous pranks.

There was always plenty of good food to eat. I especially appreciated the abundance of milk from the school's own dairy herd. Some of the boys had to care for the cows. It was their job to feed them and milk them also to clean the barns and the corrals. Other boys, however, helped do the baking or the cooking. We all had work assignments to carry out every day.

My first duty was to help wait on tables. Later, as I grew older and stronger, I was assigned to help clean, scrub halls and dormitories, then; to assist with the washing, ironing and sewing. School was very confining, even during vacation time, for all the children under 12 years old. The only time we got to go to town was when we didn't have money to spend; and outside of what fun we could get from looking in the store windows, or just looking at people, --town really wasn't too attractive.

One of the highlights, and a thrilling event of my life, was the time that my father's sister sent me a silver dollar. It was the first dollar I had every owned, and the only real money that I every received from my people all of the time I was away at school. This event has not faded into an insignificant event, when I think about the effort and the sacrifice mother made in the only way she was able to, show her deep, undying love and devotion for her little girl who was away from home, but not away from her heart!

My mother had to be both father and mother to my younger brother and her sacrifices were many. She gathered wild hay and firewood— all of which she carried on her back. How many miles she traveled or how many tons she carried, no one will ever know. The hay and wood were sold for a paltry sum of money, which was desperately needed for clothing and a little food from the store to supplement the wild food she was able to gather. Occasionally, mother would send me a package of acorns or other wild food, that she remembered I had enjoyed so very much as a little girl. This was a real treat for me and my friends since we never had grown tired of the wild food, which Mother Nature had been so wise to place on the desert in Arizona.

Once in a while she would send me a small basket, which she had made. I would sell it (for a pitifully small price) and have a little spending money. Little did I realize then, what a sacrifice it had been just to pay the postage to send the things.

My first job away from school was when I was 12 years old. It was at the Pickett Ranch right out of Grand Junction. Mrs. Pickett was a widow living with her two stepsons. She was a very wonderful person and treated me more like a daughter than an employee. She taught me how to do many things, such as cooking and keeping house. Everything was so much different than school. Though the wages in those days were just $12 a month, those dollars were the biggest dollars in the world to me. In three months I had earned $36, all my own. Even though the money was sent to the principal at the school to keep for me, it was just like having money in the bank, because I could draw a dollar or two when I needed it. I was allowed to return the following year to the Pickett Ranch and work during the vacation period. The next year I was kept at the school to cook for the employees—at no pay.

Maybe I should mention at this time that it wasn't all work and no play at school. We had a very well balanced play activity program, indoors, as well as, outdoors. The swings were a big favorite. And with lots of snow and ice during the wintertime, we had fun building snowmen, throwing snowballs, sliding on the ice, and even pushing or pulling one another on sleds.

Those of us who were selected from the graduating class of 1900 to be sent away to high school, went to three different destinations. Two others and I, one a Papago boy by the name of Joshua Ramon and the other an Apache girl, Amy Pinchelini, were sent to the Hampton Normal Institution at Hampton Roads, Virginia. There were about 150 Indians of different tribes from many states. Those from the Southwest were assigned their own table in the dining hall, the Southwestern Table.

There were well over 1000 students attending this school. Almost 900 Negroes made up the balance of the enrollment. The Indian girls were quartered at Winona Lodge. The Indian boys were quartered at the Wigwam Lodge. The Negro girls were assigned to Virginia Hall; and the Negro boys to their own hall. My room was on the fourth floor. My roommate was an Onadonga girl by the name of Adele Quinn, from Syracuse, New York. Adele was a very fine person, smart and well mannered. She was taking post-graduate work at the school and with her higher knowledge and wider experience, she helped me to understand the strangeness of eastern customs. One day, Amy P. and I accompanied two Indian boys across the river in a rowboat to get some persimmons. When we got back, the matron was waiting for us and we were in trouble. We didn't take any more trips without permission.

Routine at Hampton was quite different. We attended school only half a day. The rest of the day was for our work assignments, including doing our own laundry. We earned a small amount of spending money for the work we did. Those who did general cleaning, such as halls, dining rooms and kitchen, were paid $1.50 a month; those who did special jobs were paid $1 a month. I was one of the lucky ones. My job was to take care of Georgia Andrew's room. She was one of the teachers at the school and we became best friends.

The school secured vacation jobs for us. They sent me to Great Barrington, Massachusetts, to work for a family by the name of Smith. They had four small children. In a few days we were just one big happy family. Oh yes, the pay here a fabulous $15 a month and keep. Georgia Andrews saw that I was sent to work for her folks the next year, in the suburbs of Boston.

They also sent a Sioux Indian girl named Sybil Conger, to the same area. It was good for us to see each other once in a while, since the ways of the East were still strange to us.

One of the unusual things I remember was the colored girl who was enrolled, with the full status of an Indian, by the name of Eva Shaw. The Creek Indian Tribe had adopted her parents, and she was born on the Creek Indian Reservation in Oklahoma, having all the rights of an Indian. She also received regular royalty checks from her land allotment.

What contact I had with the Negro students, in class or on the grounds, was without question of the highest nature. They were jolly and courteous, considerate and well mannered. As far as I know, they were never involved in serious trouble the entire three years I was at Hampton.

At the end of the third term, I was allowed to return home to the San Carlos Indian Reservation with my Apache girlfriend Amy Pinchelini. Did I say home? Well, at least there was a lot of excitement when we got there. Amy found her people in a hurry; however, I did not. Some of the Apaches tried to claim me as one of their own, but they were convinced that I wasn't when they saw the Yavapai tattoo marks on my chin. So you might say that the skin of my chin saved me. Well, I was there, but there were none of my people around. I had no money to travel on. I had never been allowed to make any plans of my own. There was nothing else to do but let nature take its course. I was allowed to stay at the San Carlos School for the time being; and about this time the laundress at the school went on her 2 week vacation. I was put to work in her place, which I was glad to do for my keep.

The next break came when they sent me to Phoenix Indian School. I was getting nearer to mother all the time. One of the children in the group was Sam Russell, my sister Tha La's little boy, whom I had never heard of before. He had been left at the reservation school when my people returned to the Verde Valley. Sam did bring me up to date on a little family history. My arrival in Phoenix was very timely. I went into service as the assistant matron, while she took her vacation. My pay was some more experience and my keep. After the assistant matron returned, I was allowed to go into Phoenix and work days, doing odd jobs, washing, ironing and housework. I thought it was odd that after eleven years teaching me the three R's all I was doing was housework.

One day my mother and her brother were waiting for me out in front of the school. It was a strange feeling—we knew each other, and yet we didn't. What a wonderful feeling it was, being united again after 11 long years of separation. Mother had gotten word through the mysterious Indian grapevine that I was back in Arizona again at the Phoenix Indian School and she came for me as soon as she could. She also came to take her grandson, Sam, to spend the balance of his summer on the ranch where she and her husband were working.

It would be utterly impossible to put into words that satisfying sense of peace, security and love, which my mother constantly radiated, not only for me, but also for everyone around her. She had that rare ability to make me feel that I was really wanted as I was—right then and there. She had never attended school a day in her life, yet she was so wise in so many ways. She knew that young and old alike need to be needed, loved and understood. And that every soul has a deeper hunger than that of food.

Strangely, I had lost the ability to talk the Indian language. I could understand everything my mother and uncle said, but I just couldn't answer them other than through gestures and English. It took me at least three months to get the hang of it, before I could talk again the language of my own people, the Yavapai.

It was quite and ordeal for mother to come after me. First of all, it was a hard 2-day trip down the Verde River to Ft. McDowell, where my uncle lived. She and her husband used an unusual method of travel—the ride and walk system. Since they had but one pony, they tied a few things on the pony, then one at a time they would take turns—one would ride while the other would walk. When they arrived at Ft. McDowell, mother and her brother went for us in my uncle's wagon—another 2-day trip. All of this, just to get their grandson and "little girl of yester years". What mother would do more?

It didn't take long for me to get my things together, check out of the school and get started on my way back to be with my own people. The two-day trip to Ft. McDowell gave us the opportunity to get re-acquainted. We stayed at my uncle's place for a few days, visiting relatives and old acquaintances and making new friends. Some of the Indians couldn't talk much English, or understand it very well, so all of my "Eastern Culture" went down the drain, by way of the sign language.

The worst was yet to come. The next leg of my journey was a real test. Mother had brought a pony for me so that Sam and I could ride double up the Verde River to the Osborn Ranch, where my folks were working at the time. My mother and stepfather used the ride and walk system. It was a very rough trip. We had to cross and re-cross the river many times. The trail was rocky and over-grown with brush. Many places were very steep. A few places were so rough and steep that we had to walk and lead the ponies. Here I was a rank tenderfoot, on my first horseback trip in 11 years. Believe me, I was glad when we finally arrived at the ranch - that never-to-be forgotten day in July, 1903, very weary -- yet very happy.

It didn't take long for the Indian wireless to announce my return. Soon all of our relatives—aunts, uncles, brothers, sisters, nephews and nieces—came to see me. It was quite a reunion. Of course, they did not all arrive at the same time. Just the same, we were up to our ears in relatives most of the first month I was home. How mother was able to manage to supply the many needs created by the situation, on seemingly nothing, is something at which I shall always marvel. Her formula was simple. She would merely say, "Do the best you can, on what you have."

Our home was the familiar wikiup, in multiples to fit our housing requirements. Though far from modern, and devoid of many conveniences, they had their advantages. When we decided to move to a new location, it was a simple matter to build a new wikiup.

Possibly an important point about the Indian way of life is, that by living a simple life and by living close to nature, they could better appreciate and be thankful for all of the things that Mother Nature had to offer.

We left the Osborn Ranch about a year afterward and moved up the river to a little Indian settlement on the hills in the neighborhood of Bridgeport. This was my home for the next two and one-half years. My brothers, Ne-pa-pai-ma and Ka-thad-ah-hanna, worked at the Don Willard Ranch nearby. I also went to work there, cooking and doing the housework.

Drama was mother's life at this time. She and her husband separated. Here again, simplicity is the rule. When tension develops to the point of utter disharmony between Indian couples, the wife simple gathers the husband's belongings and places them outside of the wikiup. He knows it is time to move on. No arguments or killings needed. Both respect each other's right to live and let live, and no one is really mad at anyone. It's just a matter of using a little common sense.

Our next move was of short duration. My brothers had work at a new mining operation on the slope of Mingus Mountain. We moved there and mother and I proceeded to set up housekeeping for my brothers. Six months later, the mine was closed. When I asked my brother Ne-pa-pai-ma why, he said, "White man ran out of check book"; so we went to the Verde Valley. This time we camped at Cottonwood, a little country store and one house. But my brothers were feeling like big shots, with the few dollars they had accumulated while working and they contracted a chronic case of laziness. They did not try to find work for almost a whole year.

At night, the lights of Jerome would fascinate me. Clustered on the side of the mountain, as it is, it resembled a magnificent jewel in a giant setting, beckoning for me to come and try my luck. This I did. It wasn't difficult to find day work, mostly washing and ironing, but it was difficult to commute from Cottonwood to Jerome each day since I had to walk all of the way and it was all up hill. I had to start from Cottonwood before daylight. The trip back wasn't so bad though since it was all downhill. Mother would caution me not to carry bitterness in my heart, because it only makes the road longer and the load heavier. It took time to heed her advice, but little by little the resentment dissolved and my life started to take on a brighter hue as romance came into my life.

I met Sam Hawkins in May, 1908 and we were married in Jerome a few days later. We had an Indian wedding—no ceremony. We made our vows with the Great Spirit as our witness. Then we started a life of our own. Sam was only 18 years old and I was 23. He had never been to school; so I had to be mother, wife and teacher to him. A little boy was born to us in January, 1910. He only lived a few days. Our second son was born July 16, 1913. We named him John, but we called him Jack.

As soon as I was able to go back to work, I took the baby with me. Sam, in the meantime had eaten some spoiled food at a restaurant. He became violently ill that same afternoon and had to go home from work. When I arrived that evening, he was doubled up with pain and neither of us had presence of mind to get a doctor. He was feeling a little better the next morning, but still much too sick to go to work. Whatever it was that he ate poisoned his entire system. He kept losing weight and finally passed away May 7, 1915.

Again, I was to experience the cruelty of Indian behavior towards the widow of a dead husband. My husband's parents demanded that I turn my son over to them, to raise. One time my father-in-law even came to the house and jumped on me, and would, no doubt, have injured me seriously had I not been able to get away from him. My sister, Tha La, heard about it so she came one day and removed all of my belongings from the house and took them to my mother in the Verde Valley. I had to follow with my son. It was their way of getting me back near them so they could protect me. Even there, I wasn't too safe. My in-laws were always lurking close by just waiting for the chance to take my baby.

Somehow, a way out of every difficult situation always opens up; when one is doing what she thinks is right. I got word that some Yavapai Indians were getting ready to leave, early in June for the Exposition in San Diego, California. There was an opening for an Indian woman with a small child. I went along.

Our job was to erect an authentic Indian Village and live in it just as though we were living on the reservation. Therefore, we built our wikiup and put on the "side show" for the benefit of thousands of camera fans and curious onlookers. All of the Indians kept occupied at different tasks—grinding corn, cooking out in the open, weaving baskets, etc. It was a lot of fun and we were there about five months.

What a change five months can make in a person's life, especially when the proper ingredients are added. It was at the exposition that I became acquainted with Leonard Hayes another one of the Indian participants. We became very fond of each other and for the first time in my life, I was conscious of the fact that love wasn't a one-sided proposition and that men were capable of imparting love, a deep feeling, the same as a woman.

Leonard Hayes asked me to marry him and I accepted. We agreed to have a Christian wedding soon after we returned to Arizona in November. Leonard proved an ideal husband. He was kind, considerate and gentle to me and to my little son. The agency had allotted us a plot of land and we both went to work on it. Soon we had one of the nicest farms on the reservation. For the first time in my life I knew what it felt like to be truly happy. The events of my past life began to cease to haunt me. I wasn't afraid anymore. Life became brighter and took on a mellow and beautiful meaning. Then our daughter, Fannie, was born to us on September 7, 1916. Our second child was another girl Hazel arrived February 19, 1919. Then our son, Leonard Jr. came along April 21, 1921 and our family was complete.

Life with us must have followed along the lines of any other normal parents raising a family. We had our problems and our celebration in our community, as well as, in our lives. We usually made it a point to spend each summer in the Verde Valley with my mother. It was so much cooler than at Ft. McDowell and it also gave us a change of environment, which is good for anyone.

Construction on the Clarkdale Smelter was started in 1912 and sometime during the spring of 1915, it was put into operation. Many of the Indians in the Verde Valley moved to a little hollow just west of the town of Clarkdale so that those who were able to get jobs at the smelter would be close to work. It was during this period that mother and my two brothers moved there. It was to that place that we would go for the summers.

To get to Clarkdale from our home was quite an operation. We still had to go by wagon to Phoenix, catch the Santa Fe train through Prescott to Del Rio, transfer to the narrow gauge railroad to Jerome, transfer to the auto-stage for Clarkdale. By making good connections, we were able to get there in three days. The funny thing about it all is that we had to travel almost 250 miles in a round - about trip to reach a point roughly 85 miles.

Finally in 1924, we decided to move to Clarkdale permanently. Leonard went to work in the smelter as an assistant crane operator, and I went to work in Clarkdale doing laundry and housework for some families there, while mother took care of our children.

We were just about ready to build when the depression hit. Many men were laid off in the mine and smelter when the bottom fell out of the price of copper. Leonard was among those laid off. Fortunately, I was still able to find work in town so we didn't go hungry. Only our plans to build a better home just had to wait. Leonard went back to work at the smelter just as soon as they started full-scale operations again. With financial conditions becoming more favorable, we began making plans again since the house we were living in was nothing more than a shack and much too small for our family. This need was further impressed on us with the unexpected death of my son Jack. He caught a bad cold, which developed into double pneumonia and he died October 3, 1931. He was just a little over 18 years old. We doubled our efforts to get our house built and in 1932 we moved into our new home which has been my home ever since.

My brother and my uncle had to do most of the building of our house since Leonard was having a lot of trouble with his back. He would go to the company doctor from time to time, but the medicine they prescribed failed to give him much relief. He would feel a little better in the mornings, however, by the time his shift was over in the evening, he was in agony and completely exhausted when he got home. He stayed on the job until sometime in January

1937 when he had to give up and go to bed. But not for long—he died on February 23, 1937 of Bright's disease.

The grim reaper struck again that same year in August when my mother passed on to her reward. My world seemed to be falling all around me, yet I knew this was no time for depression; but rather a time for reflection. Actually, my problems of the moment were small in comparison to those which mother had faced, all alone and without complaining.

I had never stopped working so my work pattern went on as usual. There were still mouths to feed, clothes to buy and a thousand other things to do. I had Leonard Jr's education to think about. He was a junior in high school that fall and graduated with honors in 1940. I sent him to an aeronautical school in Glendale, California for a year, after which, he got a job at an airport in San Diego to acquire a little practical experience in aircraft repairing. After eight months he returned to Clarkdale to be with us for a while. He got a job in the smelter as a pipe fitter and boilermaker, where he worked until he became of age and was drafted into the army. Owing to his previous experience in aeronautics, he was transferred to the Air Force, took his basic training in Colorado, and then went to Florida where he received his wings in 1943. He was assigned to the Mediterranean Theater as a tail gunner on one of the big bombers. While on a bombing mission, Thanksgiving Day, 1944, the bomber crashed on the side of a mountain in a dense fog. The entire crew was killed. It was a long time before they were able to recover the bodies after that fateful Thanksgiving Day mission, but in due time they sent my son's body back to us. He was buried with full military honors at Ft. McDowell where he was born. As his beneficiary, I received the insurance money along with the pension.

After a period of visiting with friends and relatives, it was a relief to return home to have a little time to myself, to gather my wits, to do a little serious thinking, to analyze the meaning of life and death and to speculate on the meaning of war and peace.

Through the years I had worked for many white people in their homes and I really got to know them. They have their good qualities and they also have their faults. The same thing applies to the Indians on and off the reservations and also out in the world and with people of all nations. They all have their good points and their bad points. I wonder what Thanksgiving Day 1959 holds in store for the people of the world? To some, maybe a feeling of security, and to others, a feeling of despair; and to many, perhaps the fear of atomic warfare and annihilation of the human race. Can this all be because the true meaning and purpose of Thanksgiving has been forgotten? Thanksgiving Day could well become that great "Love Thy Neighbor as Thyself" event, the time for more soul searching and less faultfinding. Then, in time, the spirit of brotherhood will spread around the world. Each of us has the power to plant the seed of brotherhood in our own heart --- then, with a little tender loving care, it will grow."

Note: *Thus were the thoughts and happenings during that time period, as told by my great aunt, Maggie Hayes (older sister of my grandmother, Tha la Charley). Maggie's story was evidently written and finished by the Fall of 1959.*

CHAPTER 4
FRIEDA'S APPEARANCE

This then, is the story of the Yavapai People in the beginning and how I came to be. I first appeared in this world at the Indian Hospital in Phoenix, Arizona on November 28, 1938 ; the ninth of eleven children born to Dora Taketchera and Samuel Adams Russell --- Indian name "Waskatama". The family consisted of four sons: Levi, (who died in infancy) Daniel, Aaron and Paul, (who also died in infancy), plus seven daughters Esther, Vivian, Winona, Deborah, Elividia, Frieda (myself) and Jane. Most of my siblings were not born in a hospital, but born in the Indian Community of Clarkdale. The fault with this was that, in later years, they were asked where they were born and at what hospital, they could not answer the question. They had to get a witness who could verify their birth.

My Indian name is, "Dehonja", given to me by my father after my mother's death. It had been my mother's Indian name. My younger sister, Jane, and I were sent to live with our paternal grandmother in the Clarkdale Indian Community where I began grade school at the elementary school which still stands today just recently having been remodeled for another use. I went up to the 2nd grade there in Clarkdale and then went to Prescott to live with my father for the 3rd grade and on up to the 12th grade and eventually finished high school there in Prescott.

After high school, I wanted to go to the University of Southern California, but was told by the Indian Agent that it was too big a school for me so he sent me to Haskell Indian School in Lawrence, Kansas. After one year of that, which seemed like a repeat of high school, I asked to attend the University of Kansas which was also in Lawrence so the Bureau of Indian Affairs let me do that. After a year and a half, while attending school and working at the University Student Health Services, I returned to Arizona and attended Eastern Arizona College; and I also enrolled at Northern Arizona University during the summer.

MY FAMILY AT ASH FORK

Sam and Dora (my parents) were together during a period of time (which was during the Great Depression) when it was an extremely difficult time for everyone in America. Times were hard and jobs were scarce. My father, Sam, had taken a job with the Santa Fe Railroad while living at the Clarkdale Indian Community. What happened was that my father's brother, Joe, was hired to do the job, but he had to turn it down believing that he could not handle the job. My Uncle Joe had not gone to school or learned the English language having been hidden by our grandmother, "Moda" when the government workers were rounding up Indian children to take to Indian Boarding Schools. Therefore, our father, Sam, took the job and was one of the few lucky ones who had a steady job working for the Santa Fe Railroad during the period of the Great Depression.

My father had moved his family from Clarkdale to Ash Fork, Arizona to work for the Santa Fe Railroad. I was told that the homeless and jobless people often stopped by our home in Ash Fork seeking help. Our mother would give food to the people who came by after they had helped the family with some task— like chopping wood for our wood stove or getting water for the household to use. Despite problems of that time, this was a nice time for our family, all living together, with some of my older siblings in public school in that little town of Ash Fork. My mother took in washing to earn a little extra money, plus she would also crochet and embroider pillows cases and desk scarves. Mother also made "Yavapai Indian baskets" and sold them to tourists who came by on the passenger trains going from coast to coast. My mother, I was told, was a very talented and hard working woman always helping my father out with the support of our large family. These good, happy times would not last long though as our mother became ill and was taken to the Phoenix Indian Hospital over and over again. She was in and out of the hospital so many times with health problems that the doctors of that time could not cure. I believe that my mother must have suffered greatly.

During the period that my family lived in Ash Fork, we lived in a railroad boxcar which was provided for us by the Santa Fe Railroad for its railroad workers.

Nya Jidta – My Mother: An expert Basket Weaver; who died when I was very young, so I really do not remember much about her, which all my life has left a hollow spot. But, that gives me some insight into the plight of the Children of Single Parents.

My older siblings were in public school while the younger ones stayed at home with our mother. Living in Ash Fork, I guess the Lord was watching over our family -- living and playing near the railroad tracks every day; us little ones at home, were not injured by the trains rumbling through the tracks every day. However, our family did know of one family who lived near the tracks who had one child of theirs who was run over by a train. All the children living in that area had to cross over railroad tracks in order to get to school on the other side. One day, the train started rolling when one little girl was crawling underneath the train to get to school. The girl lived but lost her legs. How unfortunate and so heartbreaking for the parents!

Since I was one of the younger children, I do not remember too much of that period living in the railroad boxcar in Ash fork. That is sad, because that was during the time which included our mother and her caring for us children. I was too young and only know that my earliest recollection of our life in Ash Fork comes to light as "moving day". It was apparently "moving day" and there I was under the boxcar hiding from the men with the big truck who were loading our belongings from the boxcar into a big truck. Everyone was rushing around! I did not know why! I hid under the boxcar as I guess that is where I used to play often and hide when I didn't understand what was going on. Some of my toys were under there and I sat under there wondering what was happening. I stayed hid under there until someone found me and pulled me out. This was the day that our family was relocated to Prescott, Arizona. Our father had been transferred to a new job site!

LIFE AT PRESCOTT

In Prescott, Arizona, our family moved onto the Yavapai Reservation and into a rock house which was nice and cool because of the rock, high ceiling and cement floor. We must have lived there only a few months in the warm months; because I do not remember enduring the cold weather that Prescott has in the winter months. The only bad part of living in the rock house was the hornets or yellow jackets which would often make a nest right over the front and back door. We would have to open the door and run out fast in order not to get stung. Other than that, there were big pine trees to play under and a small wash nearby where my younger sister, Jane, and I would sit and play with the rag dolls which were easy to make. Or, we would just run or walk on the sand with bare feet. How good that felt! The tribal man who had been kind enough to let our family live in his rock house moved into a smaller house in the back with his dog "Blackie". This old man would take his meals at our house and after dinner, sit and talk to his dog in the Yavapai language, which the dog seemed to understand pretty well. I remember this short period as a fun time.

During this period, my mother, Dora was sick more often and not around much. She was often taken to the Indian Hospital in Phoenix where they would keep her. My father would often send for his mother, Jun Tha La, who would come to watch us kids. My father worked in the town, of Prescott which seemed quite a ways from the reservation, but he walked to and from work every day whether it rained or shined. I remember that my happiest times would be when I saw my father walking home after work carrying a grocery sack full of food for the family. How secure he always made me feel and how proud I was of him being so big and strong and caring for his family!

The reservation people there were sympathetic to our family and seeing how they were also so closely related to us, I can understand. The recognized "Chief", Viola Jimulla, of the Prescott Yavapai Tribe and her family included Viola Jimulla's daughter, Grace, who was married to my great uncle, Ed Mitchell's son, Don Mitchell. Don Mitchell worked at Fort Whipple as a security guard but also considered himself as a guard on the reservation. Chief Viola and her family members all attended the little Presbyterian Church on the reservation and almost everyone living on the reservation also attended that church -- which included our family. Of all of the Jimulla Family, my favorite was Lucy Miller. Lucy was a tall, beautiful lady with graying hair, far different in appearance from her sister Grace, who was shorter and a little on the heavy – set side. Lucy did not have any children of her own like Grace did; and she favored me—the little rag-a-muffin. She always called out to me, "Where is my Frieda Ann?" "Frieda Ann" she called me, instead of just plain old "Frieda". That is why to this day, I prefer to use my middle name along with my first name when I sign anything—remembering Lucy and how she liked me best over all the other children on the reservation!

MOVE TO CLARKDALE TO LIVE WITH MODA

As my mother, Dora, became increasingly ill and needed to be hospitalized for longer periods, old Moda (grandmother) came to Prescott to care for us for longer periods of time until it was decided that the time had come for the younger ones to go home with her to the little Indian Village near the town of Clarkdale, Arizona. The older children were sent off to boarding schools. My sister, Jane and I, were taken to Clarkdale and to our Moda's home by our Uncle Joe who came for us from Clarkdale where he lived. Our older brother, Aaron; was already living in Clarkdale with Moda. While living there with our grandmother, our mother passed away, followed by a newborn son named Paul, who was taken care of by my Uncle Joe and his wife Louise. My mother and Baby Paul were buried in the old Indian cemetery on the hill near the Indian Village in Clarkdale, Arizona. I was still so young and hadn't spent much time with my mother, I really did not know her—even to remembering how she looked, how tall she was, her personality, nothing at all. These things I was told by my older siblings. At my mother's funeral, however, I remember being lifted up by Uncle Joe, along with my younger sister on his other arm, to view the body in the casket. How sad it was that I did not really know that the woman lying in the casket was my mother.

Uncle Joe or "Nan Ja",(as an uncle is called in Yavapai) was the uncle who did not get educated due to being hidden by our Moda. However, he always managed to get work in the smelters or mines near Clarkdale and was one of the few Native Americans back then who owned an automobile. I remember I was told to put on my shoes as my sister and I had to go with Uncle Joe to our Moda's home in Clarkdale. I was usually barefoot so I ran around the rock house frantically trying to find the only pair of shoes that I had so I could get in Uncle Joe's car. Today I have made sure that I have more than one pair of shoes!

This began our new life with our grandmother in Clarkdale, Arizona. Moda raised us according to the Christian way of life. Our church was the Presbyterian Church in the Indian Community. The first preacher for the Presbyterian Church at the village, I have been told, was an Indian preacher from another reservation named Joshua Wellington who worked hard to get the church started. He lived near the church in a small parsonage with his family. My sister Winona tells of a time when she almost drowned in a flash flood which happened in the big wash at the Clarkdale Community while she was

A CHILDHOOD HERO:
ONE, WHO AS SUCH; HAS LASTED ALL MY LIFE; A TRULY GREAT ITINERANT YAVAPAI PREACHER
ANDREW JACKSON

Fond or better said "Precious Memories" of this fantastic gentle-man that Preached to us and displayed the "Love of Jesus" in the "Only Language" we all knew at that time. He was a delightful man with a wonderful sense of humor; he was always good natured and had funny stories to tell about his travels. At Christmas time he would often come around with toys for us girls and a pound of Coffee for Moda. He was a good Christian man and we were all blessed to know him.

living there with Moda. There is a big wash between the Presbyterian Church and the community houses where our Moda lived and it had to be crossed in order to get to the church. Winona said that the Indian people were skipping rocks to cross the flood and she was skipping too, even though being a small child, she missed a step and fell into the flood waters. The water coming down from Jerome was fast and very strong—Winona was swept down the wash. She thought she would drown for sure; but the preacher, Joseph Wellington, jumped into the water and pulled her out of the water. It is something that Winona never forgot. I've learned since that Mr. Wellington wanted to stay there in that community forever as he grew to love the place, but things did not work out and so he left and went back his own reservation. There were several preachers who came to Clarkdale after that; and at one time, there was a Yavapai Indian man named Andrew Jackson who traveled the Yavapai area by foot or sometimes by bus, when he had the fare, in order to do his preaching as a layman. He had been selected by the Moderator, Reverend Forrey of Prescott. Andrew Jackson preached in the Yavapai Language at the different Yavapai villages and reservations around the Yavapai territory. This preacher, Andrew Jackson, did not get a big salary so he often came to Moda's house to eat. Moda fed him and also enjoyed his company, because he would tell stories of the places he'd been and how the people at those reservations were doing. At any rate, Moda would offer her hospitality to anyone who needed it.

As I recall Andrew Jackson, I view him as a delightful man with a wonderful sense of humor. He was always good-natured and always had funny stories to tell about his travels. At Christmas time he would often come around with toys for us girls and a pound of coffee for Moda. He was a good Christian man and we were blessed to have known him!

Moda's Family

Moda had two brothers who were named "Fred and Ed Mitchell". Fred, was a bachelor, who lived in a small house next to Moda. He would always come to visit and take his meals with Moda. He was tall and slender just like Moda's other brother Ed. Fred would eat and drink coffee, then sit around afterwards rolling up those brown cigarettes, smoking and carrying on conversations with Moda late into the evening. I was always aware of his big, black shoes that tied up high on his legs which he crossed while he sat and talked for hours – in Yavapai, of course. Fred wasn't around that long as he must have passed on early in life. I didn't know what happened to him—only that one day he wasn't there anymore. Later on when I was grown, one of my cousins (Naomi, -- my Uncle Henry's daughter) talked about our Uncle Fred and said she spied on him one evening by peeking through his window. As she went on talking, I hated to hear what she might say next; but it was nothing bad. She told me that as she peered through the window of Fred's home, she saw Uncle Fred getting ready for bed and he was in his long johns. She said that he got down on his knees by his bed, bow his head and pray. I might have known that he was a believer also—how nice it was to hear that about my great Uncle Fred!

My grandmother's other brother "Ed Mitchell", also lived in the Indian Village with his wife Rena. His wife was an outspoken woman and caused my grandmother a lot of dismay. My Moda would often question her brother Ed and ask him what he saw in this woman and what made him stay with her. However, it must have been true love as the two stayed married for many, many years. I would guess that he knew how to keep his mouth shut when it was necessary.

At certain times when the Town's (Clarkdale) dump truck would come by in the village headed for the dump across the wash over by where the Mexican Village was, all the Indian village people would watch to see who would be the first to head for the dump. It was always Rena (My great Uncle Ed's wife) who would get her cane and head for the dump. All the tribal people would say under their breath, "there goes Rena—she always gets the best stuff!" At any rate, you can see that we did have some characters living on the reservation.

Sometimes, my Moda would take me and Jane to the dump with her to get stuff and we would see a lot of pigs there which belonged to a Mexican family living close to the dump. Later in life, I was told that my sister Winona would feel sorry for the pigs and their running noses and take the bottom part of her dress to wipe their noses.

UNCLE HENRY

The people in this small village at Clarkdale were mostly Yavapai at that time with just a few Apache. My Uncle Henry, who also lived close by to my Moda's house, was married to an Apache woman named Daisy Quesada, who it was said, came from Cibeque in Apache country. This lady was a half-breed woman, part White and Apache. She was a beautiful lady! She spoke Apache and learned to speak Yavapai pretty well– teaching her children both languages. She and my Uncle Henry had four sons and three daughters. There was Nathaniel, Ned, James and Bobby, the three daughters were Naomi and Agnes, and one named Henrietta, who died in infancy. Their children were a little bit older than Jane and I. Agnes was their youngest child, closer in age to my older sister Winona, as they were born on the same day! My brother Aaron and Uncle Henry's son Bobby were about the same age and attended Clarkdale High School at the same time. Their house was close by so we were all in close proximity and got to see each other every day.

I remember that my Uncle Henry had chickens and my sister Jane and I were often told to go and help find eggs as the chickens were allowed to roam all over the area. Moda's home was on the top of a small hill and below the hill was a small stream

Clarkdale

**My Uncle Henry with his wife Daisy and Children
Nathaniel, Ned, Bobby, Naomi and Aggie**

running below. There was a lot of bamboo and grass below the hill where we had to search for the eggs. Sometimes we would just run through the bamboo stalks playing hide and seek and forget about searching for the eggs. At those times, when we were playing instead of looking for eggs, we would get in trouble with our Uncle Henry.

One thing that sticks in my mind about the chickens is that one day my Uncle Henry showed us how he chopped off the heads of the chickens to get it ready to cook. Uncle Henry then proceeded to chop off the head of the chicken he had; but the chicken fell off of the table and went running around without his head. This was kind of scary to me as a little girl; but looking back on that now, I think, isn't that like a lot of people we know who run around in every direction seeming not to have a head – not really knowing where they are going or what they are doing?

MY UNCLE JOE

My grandmother's youngest son, Joe, also lived in this village, but across the creek and up another hill. He was married to a woman, named Louise, who did not bear him any children. They, however, kept and raised a boy named Lawrence, who changed his last name to "Russell" being adopted by my Uncle Joe. He was related to Uncle Joe's wife, Louise, and that was how he came to live with them. Uncle Joe and his wife also from time to time kept a girl named Phyllis

Pablo who was related to Aunt Louise also and a sister to Lawrence. They also took in other children from time to time who needed a home. There was also a Joni and Shirley Bonnaha who lived with them at one time. Uncle Joe and Louise were good, caring people – always willing to help!

My Uncle Joe recalls memories of being born on the San Carlos Reservation on June 19, 1890. That was because of the "forced internment" of the Yavapai at the San Carlos Reservation. However, he returned home when they were set free from internment. Of course, all of the other Yavapai also returned home to the Verde Valley.

This was at the turn of the century, when the Yavapai returned to the Verde Valley and tried to fit into a new lifestyle. Uncle Joe did not have an education but he always managed to get himself a job to support himself and the children who lived with him. Uncle Joe was employed on the power line project for a while. He was also employed at the Phelps Dodge Smelter in Clarkdale from 1935 to 1950. Although Uncle Joe spoke limited English, as did most of the Indians at that time; he managed to get by fairly well. I personally remember my Uncle Joe as a very kind and compassionate individual. Late in life, after his wife Louise had died, my Uncle Joe met a widow by the name of Guadalupe Lewis who was from the Acoma Pueblo in New Mexico and whose husband had passed away (Tommy Lewis). My Uncle Joe took over the job of raising her seven

Brothers:

My Uncle: Joe Russell   My Dad: Samuel Adams Russell

Nya dala gela   Nya dala

children; but later he and Lupe had one daughter of their own who was named after his mother -- my grandmother, (Jun Tha La Charley). His daughter was named "Tha La" and this daughter grew up, got married and had two daughters and one son of her own. Therefore my Uncle Joe who always loved children, late in life, had one daughter of his own and three grandchildren! How happy he would have been to know these children if he had lived longer! The children all look so very much like my Uncle Joe; and it makes me remember and miss my Uncle Joe!

Moda

Living with Moda, our meals with Moda never varied much as she usually served us fried potatoes and tortillas every day. The tortillas were made fresh every day by my Moda; and the fried potatoes always smelled so good after a long day of playing outdoors! Despite the fact that there was almost no variety in the meals that our Moda gave us, I think that even to this day, I enjoyed my Moda's meals; and I can truthfully say that fried potatoes and tortillas are still my favorite food and always will be! The meals prepared by our Moda would be put in the middle of the floor in the skillet that they were cooked in and all the family members would gather around in a circle, using a piece of tortilla as a utensil and eat right out of the skillet. Everyone took just a little. No one could be greedy as there was not that much to go around. Once in a while, we would have deer meat given to us by one of the tribal members.

I was told later when I was grown that my Moda also cooked rats (Mulka in Yavapai) which my brother Aaron said he would chase out of the bushes and clobber them when they ran out of the bushes, take them to Moda to skin, clean and boil for our dinner. I guess the rats (Mulka) were all right. I'm still alive and well!

Once a month Moda got a check to live on which was from her husband who had been a scout for the Cavalry. She would take Jane and me to town. That would be nearby, Clarkdale or Cottonwood, which were quite a distance away when you're just a little girl with short legs. She would buy potatoes, shortening, coffee and other staples. At that time too, as a treat, she would usually get us ice cream cones. In Yavapai, the ice cream cones are called "hath botch dov", which means "frozen ice". We would walk all the way to town and back again. The night after the walk, I would often get leg cramps; and I would cry and cry; whereby, Moda would get up and rub my legs for me. She would rub Vicks or Menthalatum on my legs, which was what she used for all our pains. Looking back, at life with our Moda, I know that we never had much, but we never went hungry either. Sometimes, we would go to the Verde River with Moda and pick wild spinach, which was one thing I really hated as a child. I would pretend to eat it but would always take it out of my pocket, squeeze it in my hands and throw it away whenever I got a chance.

Life with our grandmother was all right. At least we had a home. No one spoke English so everything taught to us was in our native language. Moda often told us stories of how the Indian people had not been treated right and that was why we had to live a hard life –but that we had to be strong and take what life offered us. She told us of how her tribal people were all herded up and taken to a place far away from their homeland to live. How they had to all walk there and live for years before they could come back to their homelands. She told us our Indian lands had been taken away from us so now we had only this place to live in (Clarkdale Indian Village). I wondered about what she told me and wondered how people could treat other human beings like this. I felt that there was no good in some people and that they must be a completely different kind of people who only lived to do harm to others.

Some good times with Moda were the stories that my Moda told us in the winter about a time when all the animals could talk to each other and to humans also. Those stories were stories our Moda told us at night when we were all cuddled together, warm and cozy in our Moda's bed. Those stories (Gathad La Ha/Coyote Stories) Moda told us were generally about the wily coyote and his tricks on people --and the way she told them, I felt she really hated that coyote!

[*The following Gathad La Ha stories are two of the stories Moda told us:*]

BADGER AND THE DESERT TORTOISE

Badger and Desert Tortoise set up a wrestling match after both got through boasting about how strong they were. They each thought that he was better than the other and could take the other down. Badger said he was the strongest but Desert Tortoise said the same thing! All of the people and animals heard about this argument and about the great wrestling match that was coming up between Badger and Desert Tortoise and decided that they would go see the match. When the wrestling match began, the spectators began to take sides. Some got on the side of Badger and some got on the side of Desert Tortoise. After a while, it was said that Tortoise threw Badger down. Those who had bet on tortoise said that he had thrown badger down; however, those who were betting on badger said it was not so, and that badger was only on his knees. Tortoise backers said they would not have bet had they known that Badgers backers would take that stand and lie for Badger. Badger's backers became angry and said that the backers of Tortoise were not being fair.

A fight then broke out between the two groups of spectators, -- those who supported Tortoise and those that supported Badger. It is said that since then, all living things have not been in agreement and have not lived in harmony, both animals and people. Before that, all were one, living in peace and harmony so we have the Badger and Desert Tortoise to blame for all the disunity in this world today. Everyone seems to want to fight rather than try to get along.

I think this story should teach us all something. We should at this time in life vow to learn all we can and use an educated choice when we decide on anything. We should not take sides unfairly, but learn the truth of things first. In looking toward the future, I would hope that we could all try to make a happy, peaceful place in which to live – not one of disharmony and discord that the Badger and Desert Tortoise created!

[And here is another myth or legend of our people involving the coyote.]

GATHAD LA HA

This story as told to me by my Moda tells of the coyote or the Gathad La Ha, as this is what he is called in Yavapai. I knew that the Gathad La Ha had to be a rascal and a very convincing, but foolish, foolish character. I also knew that my Moda felt total disgust for him and his shenanigans because of the way she spoke of him. The reason she felt that way is revealed in the stories she told of him and of what he did to others. This story is set in the monsoon season when the streams are running very high because of the rainfall. Well, Gathad La Ha thought he was so smart that he could fool all of the other animals. He would tell the others things with such flourish that his lies were totally believable so most of the other animals did believe him. He would try to trick them all the time because the other animals were not quite as smart as he was (or so he thought). Gathad La Ha said to the other animals: "The waters are running high and it will not be easy for you to get safely across the river. The only thing for you do is to let me swim carrying you across one-at-a-time." Although the other animals did not totally believe him and were somewhat afraid, their desire to cross the river overcame their better judgment, fears and inhibitions so they believed that Gathad La Ha would do what he said. When it came time for each of them to cross the water, Gathad La Ha said, "If you will crawl inside my body, you will stay warm and dry until we reach the other side where I will let you get out and you can join the others that are there or will soon be going over." Well, he got away with this deception for a while until one particular animal asked him for a ride across the water and Gathad La Ha agreed. However, this animal was not ready to be eaten so he pulled out his quills when they reached the other side and thus killed the Gathad La Ha. Yes, you guessed it!—This animal was a porcupine! So I guess one should remember the saying, "You can fool some of the people some of the time; but you can't fool all of the people all of the time!"

This story is like all of the other Gathad La Ha Stories in having a moral to it. We can see that we need to compare the coyote to a shyster, con artist, or someone who is just plain trying to take advantage of you. We need to be wary and use good reasoning when someone tells us to do something. In other words you do not get something for nothing so don't be fooled by a "Gathad La Ha".

These two stories are examples of what my Moda told us in the wintertime; while living in the Indian Community in Clarkdale with my Moda. However, I soon reached the age when I was told that I would have to go to school. I was taken to the Clarkdale Elementary School and left there. I did not speak English and did not even know why I was there. I guess I just stumbled around there every day until I somehow learned what was expected of me. I was quiet and shy and did not ask questions so it must have taken me quite a while to learn what to do. It was a very confusing and trying time for me. However, there were a couple of other Indian children from the village who were in school there also. One was a Charles Bonnaha, a Wilma Gibson, and an Orville Lewis, a step-son of my Uncle Joe. At home, Moda could not help me with homework or studies so it was all up to me. My brother Aaron was a little bit older and did not hang around the house much to help me with my lessons. However, I did eventually learn English and then learned to read and write. I loved reading those 'Dick and Jane" books. I would often take them home and read, and translate them to my Moda and she loved them too.

Thus, I grew up at the home of my Moda in the Clarkdale Indian Village. There were a lot of good times, going to church every Wednesday evening, church on Sunday and camp meetings in the summer time. It was always such a nice sound to hear the old church bells ringing and reminding everyone that it was time for church where most of the activities for the village occurred. Camp meeting times in the summer time were especially nice times. We all would sit outdoors under the arbor and listen to good preaching and sing good Christian songs. The village would burst with people from other reservations. When it was that time of year, we would sit outside in the evening shade at my Moda's house with Moda and other close-by neighbors and wait for the big trucks to come over the hill loaded with the Pima Indians from the Salt River Indian Reservation near Phoenix and the Yavapai Indians from the Fort McDowell Reservation near Phoenix plus several other tribal reservations in Arizona. Moda being a devout Christian took us to all the meetings. This resulted in our family members developing a strong faith and bond to religion -- for that, I am eternally grateful. Without this religious background, I would have never developed the strength I needed to sustain myself throughout life's many problems. Moda never did strike us for any reason, but was always there with plenty of love and care. She had plenty of time to talk to us about those things which we needed to know later on in life. How lucky we were to have had Moda!

I can also remember sitting outside Moda's house in the evenings on large empty cans used for stools. We could see the Indian people walking home from town on the hill across the way. We would guess at who those persons were walking on that hill. We were usually joined by my Moda's sister Maggie Hayes and her daughter Fannie or Hazel who lived just a couple of steps away. They would all sit outside talking until it got dark. Sometimes my Moda would see lights on that hill and say that there were spirits walking around on that hill, but that they must be carrying flashlights because she could see lights. I have often since wondered why the spirits needed flashlights.

Moda was physically tall and a strong heavy-set woman. She was quiet by nature; but was always quick -- witted. If you teased her about anything, she could come back real quick with a smart answer. Her subtle sense of humor was so delightful. I feel that this trait is strongly reflected today in my only daughter, Sherrilee; although Moda died (Year 1959) so many years before my daughter was born (1975) and my daughter, Sherrilee never knew her. One incidence with Sherrilee which reminded me of my Moda was when, while living in an Albuquerque trailer park, my husband Dale remarked about the speed bumps (how many there were and how if you hit one too fast and too hard, you probably would get airborne and come down on the other side of the next speed bump); and Sherrilee (or "Doe" as we call her) was riding in the car with us remarked real quick, saying that, -"that wouldn't work, I tried it already!". She said it so calmly and so quickly that it reminded me of my Moda--how quick -- witted my Moda used to be!

Our family has only a few pictures of Moda that enables the younger family members to be able to know what she looked like. Moda did not like to take pictures as she, like a lot of the other Native American people, believed that the camera would take your spirit out of your body. They did not want this to happen so they preferred not to have their pictures taken. However, a photographer for the Arizona Republic got a picture of Moda with one of her great grandchildren on her lap during a camp meeting in Clarkdale and so we do have that picture of her taken out of the Arizona Republic. My Moda did not look at the camera but looked away when the picture was taken.

While living with Moda also, we attended the small Presbyterian Church that was on the Clarkdale Indian Community. Moda was a member of that church and attended regularly. She was a devout Christian who would not miss Wednesday night bible study, Sunday morning church service, Sunday evening church service, camp meetings in the summer time or any church function if she could help it. This meant that we, her grandchildren living with her, would not miss it either. We were expected to go to church with her while we were living with her. There was never any disrespect shown to her, whatever she said was what we did. Too bad that is not the case now days. Children now days like to respond when asked to do anything, "Not now, I'm busy, or "Later", or some other excuse, which is not good nor is it very respectful. That was not the case in the good old days!

That is how my beginnings with Christianity began as a small child living with my Moda. I learned a lot about the teachings of the bible and how to live according to God's Will. Somehow, sitting next to Moda in church on those hard benches as a small child, -- teachings from the bible entered my heart. Even though I seemed to be inattentive at times, I was actually hearing what was being preached. The teachings from the bible always remained in my heart and kept me going when things got tough and unbearable throughout my life. I knew that I always had the Lord to lean on. **He** has always been my rock and strength throughout my life and I know that **He** will be with me always and even up to the end, and forever! This is a peaceful thought to have!

Moda's husband and the father of her three sons had passed away early on and she remarried. Her second husband, Yuma Charley, was, from what I

The "Apache Kid"—A Yavapai named "Yuma Charley"

learned, a good man. Yuma Charley took over the job of raising Moda's three sons, (Henry. Sam, and Joe Russell) and, it was said, he always treated them fairly. I did not know him, but I was told of his kindness and the good job he did in taking over as a stepfather to Moda's three sons.

This man, "Yuma Charley", (Moda's husband), was known to historians as who it seems was sometimes called "The Kid". Although a loving, kind man to Moda and her sons, he was at times thought to be one of the worst outlaws in Arizona Territory – known to some as The Apache Kid". He was wounded but somehow found the strength to return to Peeples Valley in Yavapai County where he often worked and to the ranch belonging to Charley Genung where he later died.

"The actual story of "The Apache Kid" began, when Al Seiber, Chief of Scouts at the San Carlos Indian Reservation, appointed a young Indian, thought to be a Yavapai also called "The Kid" to the rank of sergeant.

The Kid dressed neatly in white man clothes which had no emblems to confirm his tribal identity. His scouting skills were unsurpassed as he had proven himself in many pursuits of renegades which included Geronimo. Seiber appointed The Kid to "Chief of Scouts" when Seiber left on an inspection tour.

Everything went along fine for The Kid until the summer when things happened to change his life forever! Some Apaches had got a hold of a large amount of liquor and became very rowdy. The Kid was ordered to take some scouts to the Apache camp and head off any trouble. Things went wrong when the army scouts joined the Apaches in their drinking and did not return to the fort. When Seiber learned of this, he sent troops to bring in the scouts but a situation arose and someone fired shots. They did not know for sure who fired the shots but The Kid was arrested and so were the three other scouts who were with The Kid. They were all charged with a ten year sentence in an Ohio prison. However, the U.S. Supreme Court decreed the Indian scouts were falsely tried and released The Kid and the members of his patrol. Al Seiber ignored the Supreme Court's decision and swore out warrants against the scouts so they were put back in irons within three days.

Another trial was held and Seiber named The Kid as the one who fired the shots. Even though The Kid told them that he did not fire the shots besides the fact that the Indian scouts were unarmed, and too, there was support from witnesses, the court charged the scouts as guilty. The former scouts were then ordered to be taken to the Yuma Territorial Prison in Yuma, Arizona.

Sheriff Glenn Reynolds, Deputy Hunky Dory Holmes and a man named Gene Middleton set out for Yuma, Arizona with ten prisoners. Among them were the four former scouts, five other Indians, and a Mexican embezzler -- all who would never reach their destination. What happened then was that on the second day of the trip, eight handcuffed prisoners were ordered to ease the load on the horses by getting out and walking up a steep hill. The Kid and a former scout named Hoscalte, who were considered the most dangerous of the group, were to remain shackled and remain in the wagon. Near the top of the hill, it was believed that there was a signal which passed between the prisoners who were walking by the side of the wagon. The prisoners overpowered Sheriff Reynolds and Deputy Holmes and killed the two men. The prisoners then freed the two former scouts who were still shackled and still in the wagon. By November 2, 1889, every sheriff's office in Arizona was notified and troops from several forts were ordered for the manhunt of these escaped prisoners. The escapees were all caught and killed within four months except for "The Kid". From that time on, every crime committed in the territory was blamed on "The Kid" whether they knew for sure that he did it or not.

However, "The Kid" was never seen and so they thought he might be dead. Yet, on February 27, 1893, the Territorial Legislature increased the reward money for "The Kid" from $1,000 to $6,000. The Yavapai knew that "The Kid" was around and Charley Genung on whose ranch he had come back to knew also that "The Kid" had returned by listening to the Yavapai men talk about him. The story of "The

Kid's" tragic and sad end had never been told before because it was locked away in the pages of Charley Genung's writings for years.

Charley Genung had learned from the Yavapai that "The Kid" had returned to the area near his boyhood home from Mexico because he was suffering from ill health. Charley was tempted to go for the reward money so he rode to the camp where it was said the fugitive was and spotted a figure in the bushes who he felt was "The Kid" but he rode off not wanting to be a target. However, the next day, the same Indians he saw the day before came to his ranch and with "The Kid" who appeared to be very ill. Some of the men tried to convince Charley Genung to capture "The Kid" while he was there, but he would not; because he could see that "The Kid" was dying. "The Kid" didn't appear to have long to live so they left him alone. Three weeks later, one of the Indians from the settlement at Congress, AZ was cutting wood for Charley when Charley asked him if "The Kid" had come by. The Indian answered "yes" and then was asked where he was. The Indian replied that he had died. He was asked what was done with him and the Indian said they covered him up. When they were asked where they buried "The Kid", they said, "About a foots" was the answer. That was all that Dan Genung's grandfather would say concerning the death of the "Apache Kid", who, it turns out, was Yavapai, -- not Apache! These words were so true!" (Claremont, California-based Dan B Genung, Jr., a retired clergyman, was born in Prescott, Arizona, a third generation Arizonan.)

Even though there seems to be a great mystery about Yuma Charley and who he really was, one tribal member (now deceased) "Lefty" (Leonard Harris) remembered and recalled a time when growing up in the Clarkdale area, how Yuma Charley gave Lefty his first donkey when Lefty was eight (8) years old. Lefty recalls that Yuma Charley was married to a woman who lived in Clarkdale who, I believe, was my Moda. Lefty recalled that Yuma Charley was the Indian scout who was part of a group who met up with Geronimo in Northern Mexico during negotiations for Geronimo's surrender.

Lefty also recalled the name that he gave to his donkey which was "Jinnie"; and that he was never supposed to leave the donkey on his own according to what Yuma Charley had told him or he would come back and take the donkey back. However, he did just that when Lefty was sent to Albuquerque Indian School --unwillingly. Lefty would never see his "Jinnie" again after that. Another resident of the Clarkdale area an Apache lady remembers the large herds of burros in the Cottonwood area. She said, "The Clarkdale group of Indians would go over to Cottonwood and steal some of the burros. A few days later, the Cottonwood group would come to Clarkdale and steal their burros back."

That was the life of my step-grandfather, Yuma Charley or "The Apache Kid"—who, I believe, was really a Yavapai, and who helped my Moda raise her three sons -- Henry, Sam and Joe. Russell. *Later on, of course, Moda helped to raise all of the grandchildren belonging to her son Sam when his wife, my mother, Dora Taketchera, became ill and died at a young age. This is a job that Moda took over willingly with a lot of love for the children. I don't think any of us children ever look back at that time we spent with Moda without love and fondness for the grandmother who was there for us when we needed her.*

During that period also, the federal government would often go to the Native American settlements and take the children who were of age to go to the government boarding schools which were usually located some distances from the children's homes. The children, I imagine, must have been very afraid having been forced to go to strange places, not having their parents near them, and all the while trying to learn a new concept of living and not even having mastered English yet!

My Moda had one sister named Maggie Hayes. I am proud and happy to say that I knew my Moda's brothers and sister. Maggie Hayes, was Moda's older sister and she lived just a few steps away from my Moda's house in the Clarkdale Indian Community. Living close by, she would visit often. I remember her two daughters, but I did not know her sons who died early on.   Maggie kept a tight rein on her youngest daughter, Fannie, who was not allowed to grow and blossom – instead, she became a "dependent person". When Fannie was younger, she would often talk to my Moda about one day having a home of her own with windows all around so that if there was a fire, she could just climb out in any direction and be safe.   Sadly enough to say, that Fannie never married or left her mother's home. When her mother Maggie Hayes passed on in later years, (the family was living in Ft. McDowell at that time)   Fannie could not take care of herself so she was taken to one of her relatives to live with her. Her relative (Ethel Pilcher in Fort McDowell) took her in and took care of her until Fannie died years later.

I remember also Maggie's older daughter, Hazel, who lived with an Apache man at Maggie's house. This man's first name was "Bennie" and he was a drunk and very abusive to Hazel, and even more so, when he was drinking. At those times, my Moda would take my sister Jane and me into the house and latch it with a wooden latch which probably wouldn't have held if that man decided to break into that house. My brother Aaron, who was just a young boy, would run off to a neighbor's house until the police were notified in the Town of Clarkdale. Having no phones, it would take a while for the police to be notified and respond. Sometimes, this man, Bennie, would have a gun and just shoot it off blindly in any direction— lucky he did not kill anyone with his wild shooting.

What a horrible person he was! The worst thing though that Bennie did was to beat on my cousin Hazel whom I thought was a very pretty woman. Ahead of her time according to the Indian ways, Hazel dressed very modern. She often wore high heels to events and used makeup which most of the other Indian women did not do at that time. Hazel lived with this man many years and took the beatings often which proved very detrimental to her later on in life. The beatings got to her and she became disoriented. She could not function and was taken to a mental hospital where she spent the rest of her life - never coming home. She died in that institution which is so horribly sad to think about! Years later, when my brother Aaron was grown, he saw Bennie at an Indian Doings, and walked up to Bennie, remembering the way Bennie treated our cousin, my brother Aaron walked up to Bennie and knocked him flat—which we all thought Bennie greatly deserved!

My great aunt, Maggie Hayes at one time wanted to raise me and asked my Moda if she could take me into her home as she did not have any grandchildren. My Moda agreed because she had plenty of kids to care for so my few belongings were taken to Maggie's house. It was different being totally cared for and watched throughout the day. However, I missed my siblings who were just a few steps away; and I would often wander back to them and to Moda's house. Maggie realized that I probably should remain with them so she took me back to my

Moda's and that ended my stay with Maggie – whether I would have had a better life with Maggie is not known. However, I just knew that I wanted to be with my Moda and siblings so that is where I stayed.

BACK TO PRESCOTT

I was ready to enter the 3rd grade when Moda took Janie and me to Prescott to visit our father Sam, who was working there and living in an old house near the Santa Fe Railroad. The house was made up of two small houses, a rundown garage, an abandoned chicken coup and an outhouse all on top of a small hill, below which ran Granite Creek. The two-room house had a porch, a kitchen and one bedroom. The other house, not connected, had a bedroom and a tiny room which may have been a closet, but which could be used for a small bedroom. The house must have looked pretty shabby to others, but I thought it looked pretty good. There were cottonwood trees and walnut trees nearby to play under in the summertime. There was a dirt road that separated the house from the Prescott Power Plant which supplied electricity to the town. A road wound around the property to the Mexican village which was called "Old Ball Park" at that time. A lot of the town's Mexican population lived in that area which had houses much like my dad's except that they had electricity and running water. This is where we found my father. It was good to see and be with our father again. He, a kind, gentle man, soft spoken too, was also a devout Christian man. Jane and I stayed

▲ __Home in Prescott:__ ▲
Janie – Virginia (*step-sister*) – Elividia and Me

Prescott in the Snow:
Virginia, Annie (*step-mother*) – Janie and Me

Life in Prescott
our formative years

Winona and Deborah
just sisters standing tall.

Jane, Elividia and ▲
Winona; Good kids,
happy sisters.

Vivian and Winona ▶
Pleasant young

After Graduation "Photo Op" ◄ and "Stress Relief": Happy to say "I did this", and now I'm ready to face whatever comes my way. I have Proof now that I'm worth something; having others tell me that, helped; but this is "Proof".

Below are pictures of me relaxing close to our "Prescott Home".

Frieda Ann Eswonia

Graduation Day: Class of 57

Prescott High School, Prescott, Arizona

My Graduation Dress that I will always cherish the memory of; because I had accomplished something and the dress was a gift from my wonderful school counselor.

The "Rite of Passage": In my view of myself; this was an important day. And the pride shown by my family is a great memory.

with our father in Prescott. Our Moda went back to Clarkdale alone. She did however, have our older brother, Aaron, who stayed with Moda in her home and finished high school in Clarkdale while living with her. Jane and I were back in Prescott to live with our father and we attended public school there. We also attended a small church which was the Presbyterian Church on the Yavapai Reservation. To me, being young and smaller, it seemed quite a ways out of town at that time. Sometimes we girls (Jane, cousin Virginia at times, my sister Elividia and I) would head for church on the reservation and instead end up beyond the reservation near Ft. Whipple just playing around. My Dad would hear about the times we didn't make it to church and we would be in serious trouble. Our father was stern but fair and just concerned that we should behave and not get into any trouble.

We were the only Native American family living in the "Old Ball Park" area which was located on the "wrong side" of the railroad tracks. Although we were just across the street from the power plant, we used coal oil lamps at night and carried pails to the nearest faucet we could find to get water for our household needs—sometimes faucets located at the power plant or to some Mexican house where they would let us use their water. Once we were using water from a well located in the creek bed but saw salamanders swimming in the water so we switched our watering hole. Later on, our father asked a Mexican family if he could help pay their water bill and use their water for our needs and they agreed. This made it a little easier for us, but we still had to carry buckets to their house and fill it with water and then carry it home. The buckets of water got very heavy when full of water and it was not easy for us.

There was a creek that ran below the hill where we lived and drunks usually inhabited that area. In the rainy season, the creek below our house would flood. This creek which was called, "Granite Creek" would flood its banks and people living on the other side of the road would have a hard time crossing that particular area. We would sit and watch the cars and bet on which ones would make it across the water. One time it was my older sister, Esther, who was trying to cross the flood in her car. We didn't think that she would even try it and would instead back up and go around the long way. However, much to our surprise, she came on forward and crossed without a problem and we all cheered for her.

Whatever the faults of that home, the family lived in this house for many years with our dad while he was working for the Santa Fe Railroad in Prescott. Our Dad would load and unload freight on the boxcars. Our family, at that time, consisted of myself, my sister Jane, most of the time, but at times our other siblings lived there too. There was my brother Daniel, at times my other sisters, (Winona, Deborah, Elividia), or at times my brother Aaron would come to visit from the service (Navy) or wherever he was working when he got out of the service. My sister, Vivian; would sometimes come from Los Angeles where she lived with her family to visit at times. Vivian was married to a Filipino man and had six children – three girls and three boys (Vicky, Marcelina, Patricia, Marty, Leonard and James). Our older sister, Esther too was away from home with her family in Flagstaff, Arizona. Esther had finished college and worked as a teacher and we were all so very proud of her. However, when her husband, Eddie Scott, Sr., a Hopi Indian, died in an accident, she and her family, consisting of three sons (Eddie, Jr., Courtney, and Gary) and two daughters (Luvette, and Novalene) moved to Prescott to be near the family. Time marched on and Jane and I were in grade school and then went on to Jr. High School and then to High School there in Prescott. Since we were the only Indian family living in the area, many times some of the Mexican children and sometimes their parents in this area would often call us names such as: "dirty Indians" or "dumb Indians", and "other bad names in Spanish which we quickly learned and hurled back at them. Thus, those were the first Spanish words we learned – a lot of bad words!

SAMUEL ADAMS RUSSELL

The head of my family, as I mentioned before, was our father, Sam, who was one of the three sons born to JunTha-la Charley (Our Moda). Sam was taken from his mother at an early age to the Indian Boarding School in Phoenix, Arizona. He learned

English and went up to the elementary school level. In school, they taught him a trade – he learned how to cook and bake and did just that when taking care of his family. He spoiled us with the mincemeat pie he made during the holidays and the fresh baked rolls he also made for the holidays. He loved to cook and would not trust any of his daughters to do the cooking. That is my excuse for saying that I do not know how to cook well because I was never "allowed" to cook. On Sundays usually, he made pancakes from scratch or biscuits to eat with our eggs for breakfast – how lucky we were!

My father, Sam, was Moda's middle son, and he was a tall, strong, handsome man. He could communicate in English fairly well, but preferred to speak in the Yavapai language, most of the time. He knew he had to fit into this new culture and so he did what he could in order to provide for his large family so that we could get a good start in this new era. He was a good, steady, dependable provider and especially was a good Christian man. He did not go for alcohol as so many of the Native Americans do. He often talked about one of his relatives who, was a heavy drinker, saying that all this man did was cry when he got drunk. My Dad said that didn't make any sense to drink and then cry about everything. My Dad set us an example to follow about not drinking because; as he said, drinking did not lead anywhere. Yes, my Dad was a good man and worked tirelessly at his job involving this main train route from the East coast to the West coast. This position, he held for all of his working years and retired after 38 years while stationed in Prescott, Arizona.

DORA RUSSELL

The family has several pictures of our mother ("Jiđa" as it is said in Yavapai) and she looks like a petite woman with nice facial features. She was a small woman but (I am told) a very hard - working woman. I do not know much about my mother's family (Taketchera) who were Yavapai from the Fort McDowell Reservation; and I do not know how she became a Christian. I did hear though that she was a wonderful Christian person – someone I wish I knew more closely. *I envy my older siblings because they knew her and I didn't.* I know that she raised all her children with Christian love and taught them all about the Word of God. I heard she loved to sing and would often sing Christian hymns while doing her household chores. I heard also that she could speak Spanish very well and had many Hispanic friends especially in and around Belen, New Mexico where she visited often. She was able to do this because my Dad had a railroad pass which enabled the family to travel on the passenger trains.

Both my parents, in fact, being very religious taught all their children the Christian way of life. Therefore, even though it was a trying period to live through, having faith as a Christian Family, helped our family through the bad times of the Great Depression. Our family always had food to eat and, best of all, we had each other!

<u>Nya Jidta – My Mom</u>
Dora (Taketchera) Russell
With: Brother Aaron and Sister Vivian

SAMUEL ADAMS RUSSELL
Nya Dala -- My Father, Dad, Spiritual Leader,
Provider, Role Model and more.

AARON and DANIEL

My brother Aaron was fourth eldest in our family. Like some of the others in our family, he attended public school in Ash Fork during the time that we lived there in the boxcar. I heard that he loved to make kites out of old newspapers and then fly them. One time during the school year, the children were asked to enter kites for a competition and, of course, Aaron wanted to try his luck so our mother told her older son, (my brother Dan), to help his younger brother. She told him that, being older, he was always to help the younger brothers and sisters. My brother Dan agreed and helped Aaron build a kite from our Dad's old newspapers. Well, Aaron went to school with the newspaper kite, flew it, and ended up winning first place in the competition—how happy he must have been! That is the way our older brother Dan was taught to always be there for his siblings—which he was all of his life.

Our Dad was busy with work – never got sick much so he was generally always at work every single day. He loved his sons though – and, he liked to call Aaron, "Aaron Howard" which was Aaron's middle name; and I imagine that he must have relied on Dan, the oldest son for a lot of help with the family.

Of all the children, I believe that maybe my mother was closest to her eldest son, Dan, on whom she relied on for a lot of help and, how I later learned, she would often tell him that he was her "little man" and needed to be dependable so he could help her, as

Former Tribal Chairman

Former Tribal Councilman

<u>Aaron Howard Russell</u>
Nya Waga – My Older Sibling; has been involved with the Tribal
Government for many years and is one of the most dependable
people this Tribal Nation has seen.   **<u>US Navy – Veteran</u>**

well as, the rest of the family. Daniel, who preferred to be called "Dan", or my sister Winona, or anyone of the older children were usually chosen to accompany our mother on her long trips into Phoenix by way of the railroad when she became ill. She must have relayed to them a lot of her thoughts, ideas and dreams. Even today, I believe that this position was special and that I wish that I had known my mother, as well as, the older children in order that I would have something to remember her by -- which has often been a low point in my life. I have missed my mother all my life and look forward to meeting her one day when it's my turn to leave this world.

Since my sister, Jane and I wanted to stay in Prescott with our father, Moda went back to Clarkdale alone; but our older brother Aaron was still living with her there. He said, at one point, he was enrolled in an Indian School located in Camp Verde—then later went to public school and graduated in Clarkdale before he went into the Navy. Jane and I, lived with Dad in Prescott and began public school. I was painfully shy and had a hard time with math classes, but always did well in English and reading classes. My teacher in third grade had no patience and disliked me because I did not understand math. She would make me stand at the blackboard for hours trying to do math and yet did not explain to me how it should be done. However, I loved to read every chance I got. I guess it's a good thing that we didn't have television in those days! My younger sister

Jane also started school there and so we began our life with our Dad. In Yavapai, we call our father, "Dala".

Jane and I, in our time of happiness at reunion with our father did not give any thought to our grandmother. But, isn't that the way it usually is with everyone? We forget so soon how someone has been kind to us and go on with life as if we never needed anyone – how sad that is! I often reflect on how I should have gone back and visited Moda more often. Why didn't I remember all the fun times and the love and caring that she gave me?

Schoolwork became easier and easier for me as I always studied hard. I did not fool around much, being quiet and paying attention most of the time. While the other children talked and visited with their friends, I sat quietly and did all my studies and homework. I made very good grades and enjoyed school.

However, there was that ugly problem of prejudice concerning some of the Mexican children and me. Some of them called me names and chased me around. And, it was mostly the boys who harassed and picked on me. However, the girls were different. I did have a special Mexican girl friend at that time whose name was Virginia Hernandez. Virginia was light-skinned, not like the other Mexicans who were as dark skinned as me. Virginia had pretty hazel eyes and was so special to me. We would go to her home sometimes where her mother would give us tortillas for snacks and then we would walk to the public library downtown to check out books to read. We'd take those books to my house, sit outside on the woodpile and read those books until she had to go home. I remember her to this day for being so kind to me. Virginia's family moved away before she entered Junior High and I did not see her for a long time.

Later on in life, however, I did run into Virginia in a store in downtown Prescott shopping. I had my firstborn son, LeRoy, Jr. whom I was carrying in my arms. He was about 15 months old; but Virginia was walking with her firstborn who was about seven or eight years old. We talked for a little bit and she said she had moved to a mining town nearby, but since then, I have never seen her again.

Besides Virginia, there was Carmen Granillo, a Mexican girl, who was also kind to me and, also a very pretty girl like Virginia. I met her also once in downtown Prescott. She was working in a department store where I went to buy some clothes for going back to college. I was in college then and I talked to her for a little bit. I have never seen her again since then as I did not return to Prescott very often.

One other close friend of mine was a white girl named Carol Piper. She and I would also walk to the public library and check out books to read which we would read sitting on the top of our woodpile. She had a baby brother and sometimes we'd walk to her house and go inside to see him sitting in his crib. I didn't have very many friends but the ones I had were worth a million! We also didn't have much to do – like, no television or stereos, but we did manage to enjoy ourselves. We were just happy when the library would offer us some of their old books that we could take home and keep for our own.

My sisters and I started playing baseball when our Dad made us a bat. He spent days working on that bat and we were always asking him what he was making but he would not say. Then one day it was finished and he gave it to us so we could play ball. Sometimes there were four of us girls at home and we would play with our fielders in the dirt road near our house. The Mexican girls across the way also had a lot of girls (the Espitia's) so they would come over and we would play ball. Their mother often made tamales and our dad would buy them and they were so good! I guess in those days meat wasn't quite so expensive so the tamales they made always had big chunks of meat in them; and I am a meat lover!

There was only one other Native American in my classes and he was from the Prescott Yavapai Reservation. He would tease me now and then, such as picking up my pencil or paper from my desk and move it to someone else's desk; and I would have to get up and chase him. I was told that we were related which really wasn't true.

I believe that a lot of prejudice that we experienced then was because of the movies of that period. There were a lot of movies about the U.S. Cavalry and how they killed the "hostile" Indians. When all the Indians were slaughtered, the kids would all applaud – but guess how I felt?? Most of the children spent their time at the theaters on weekends watching these movies where I feel they picked up on this kind of hatred. Indians were portrayed as "wild savages" who deserved to die. In those days, even my sister and I could afford to go to movie theaters; because it didn't cost very much and candy and popcorn included did not add up to much. My sister and I spent a lot of time watching those continuous shows when we could afford to go. My hero was "Hopalong Cassidy" who played in western movies with a black cowboy outfit and whom I thought was so handsome even with his white hair.

Summers in Prescott were nice. My sister and I would spend hours sitting on the beautiful, green grass at the plaza in town watching people go by. We would also walk to the ballparks and watch baseball games or play on the playground swings. Fourth of July times were especially nice with so many people coming to Prescott to watch the annual rodeo and other festivities. There would be parades and happenings at the plaza plus the rodeo and all its excitement. Sometimes there were three of us girls,

Jane, me, and our cousin Virginia. She would come with her mother, Annie, who was my father's girlfriend. In actuality, she was the younger sister of my mother who had passed away. They lived in Ft. McDowell, but would come occasionally. Annie also had an older daughter who only came once in a while. There was also her grown son Ernest who would come once in a while also.

Our father eventually married Annie and she became our step mother. Virginia's age was just between my sister Jane and me. She was real outgoing and a lot of fun. We didn't see much of Annie's two older children as they were older and out on their own. I do remember one time when my younger sister Jane was screaming around the house because my older sisters, being home for the summer, were teasing her; Ernest (in Prescott to visit his mother) came up to me and told me to get Janie ready and he would take her and I to the movie theater. What a nice guy I thought as he didn't want my little sister to be teased, nor did he want her to be crying. I know my brothers and sisters resented this woman and gave her a lot of problems; because they remembered our mother and wanted no one to take her place. The relationship between my dad and Annie was stormy and never worked out so it was that they eventually separated. Personally, I liked Annie and never gave her any problem as I thought she was all right. However, Annie left and my father never re-married. Remembering this relationship, I feel that we all should have left them alone as my father was happiest when she was around and it was their life to live. We shouldn't have interfered in their life.

Annie's oldest daughter, Zina, usually not around much did not cause us much concern. However, something happened, which caused Annie's son Ernest to be around for a while. One day Annie in a particularly bad mood was arguing with one of my older siblings and Ernest intervened on our behalf. He felt so badly about this (having to argue with his mother) so he left and joined the Army. My brother Aaron had already joined the Navy and had been in there since he graduated from high school. My brother Dan was drafted and also was in the Army. This was during the Korean conflict. While in the Army and in combat, Ernest was parachuting with others when he was shot down. He described to us girls later how awful it felt to lie there and have his insides come out as he was trying hard to push everything back into his body. Ernest was rescued and was eventually flown back to San Francisco and treated for his injuries there. I remember going with Annie to visit him in San Francisco. Andrew Jackson, the lay preacher, was able to drive us there to visit him. Going into that hospital full of injured soldiers was something very hard for me as a young girl. My poor cousin was paralyzed and would never walk again!

Ernest eventually though got out of the hospital and had bought a car that he could operate with his hands. He got around and was never in a bad mood as I can recall. However, he did start drinking a lot of alcohol to forget his problems and ballooned up quite a bit. I remember one time he took us girls for a ride out in the country and we had car trouble. Coming back to Prescott on the highway from Ash Fork, we had a flat tire and Ernest pulled over to the side of the road. My cousin Virginia and I stood out on the highway and flagged down a semi-truck. When the one semi-truck stopped, another semi-truck stopped also, but he was sent on his way. The driver asked us what was the matter and we told him we had a flat tire. We opened the trunk for him to get out the spare and he saw Ernest's wheel chair in there. Our flat tire was changed and we offered him what money we had, but the truck driver would not take it. What a kind white man, I thought to myself, -- so there were people who were kind and caring.

I loved my cousin Ernest as he was a soft spoken guy and always kind and considerate. He was fluent in Yavapai and preferred to talk in Yavapai. We girls would take turns taking care of him and pushing him in his wheelchair. Sometimes he stayed in Prescott and sometimes at Ft. McDowell where he eventually died from medical complications and drinking too much. We all felt so bad about his death and wondered why he, as the kindest of his family, had to be the first to go and yet his whole life was ahead of him.

Living in Prescott, we often went to the Yavapai Reservation to attend the small Presbyterian Church there which was quite a long walk from our home. Sometimes, when going to church out there, we would take a little detour which would get us clear behind the reservation and we would just spend our time climbing rocks and trees. One time, we even got a hold of some paint and painted the big boulders with our initials and someone we had a crush on. I guess this was our first graffiti. The tribal members were very upset about our artwork and our father got all the blame. Whenever our father found out about these forays of ours he would warn us that we'd better stay on the path next time and get to church like we were supposed to. Our father attended church regularly, was a loyal tither, and an elected Elder of the Indian Presbyterian church. When we missed church, our father was told and he'd make sure we made it to church the next time.

Going to church in Prescott we met a white woman by the name of Barbara Candee who, along with her mother and father, were missionaries in Christ. Barbara was tall and kind of homely, but a beautiful person anyhow. Her parents were also such a blessing to us. They taught us a lot about Christianity. They had a black van that they used to come to our home and pick us up to take us to church, or to their home for bible studies, or just to have dinner at their home, or maybe to take us to a nice picnic lunch somewhere. Sometimes we would be spiteful and hide when Barbara came over. We didn't know then how their teachings would benefit our lives. When we'd see Barbara knocking at our door, we'd all run and hide and she would have to take whatever kids she could find. Of course, we did not realize this, at that time, how good she was for us, but now I think back and wish I had gone back at some point in my life to thank her and all the others who cared enough to come around and teach us the word of God.

While living and working in Prescott, our father had a railroad pass to travel to places that was on the route of the Santa Fe Railroad. We could go all the way to Chicago on the East Coast or to Los Angeles on the West Coast. We usually went to Los Angeles, when we could, during the summer months to visit our older sister Vivian and babysit her children. She had married a Filipino by the name of Alejandro Caling and they had three sons and three daughters. Vivian and Alex were so kind to us and always would try to see that we had fun when we visited them. They knew how poor we were and did their best to see us have fun while we were with them. They would take us to the zoo, movies, the beach, parks – just anywhere they thought we would have fun; and we in turn, would help care for the children. I always enjoyed these times with my sister Vivian and Alex and their children.

Anyhow, on one trip my younger sister Jane and I went to Gallup, New Mexico to visit our sisters

Deborah and Winona and Carmen who lived there at that time; and then we were headed across to Los Angeles to visit Vivian in California. The train got to Flagstaff and made a stop. Jane and I decided to get out and go into the railroad station. While we were in the rest room, we lost our wallet – it was actually picked up by a Navajo woman who was in the bathroom also. Since we did not have our wallet or our pass, we knew we could not get back on the train. Since we could not get back on the train, we decided that we had better start walking to our Dad's home at Prescott! I don't know how many miles that is, but we were young and thought we'd make it in no time I guess. It was wintertime and there was some snow on the ground. We had our winter coats on so we decided to take off down the highway and go through Sedona instead of Ash Fork. As we started walking it was late in the afternoon and soon began to get dark. We figured that we didn't want some stranger to pick us up so we would hide every time a car came by which wasn't very often. Well, it got dark and we were getting tired so we decided to head to the side of the road and rest under some pine trees. We curled up on the ground, under some trees, when suddenly we heard something snort. We didn't know if it was a bear or a deer or what. My sister Jane jumped up and took off running down the highway like a streak. I was far behind her and I shouted to her to wait for me and she finally realized how far back I was and waited for me. We started off together again and finally made it to the winding road near Sedona where we would cut across some places and then went on down the road. At the bottom, we walked along the highway again and it must have been very late. A semi-truck came along, slowed and stopped. We were tired and eager to ride so we climbed into the truck. That was my first ride in a semi-truck. There was the driver, and Jane and I. The driver asked us if our boyfriends had dropped us off down there and we told him we had walked from Flagstaff, but he did not believe us until he asked us how old we were. We were not yet old enough to care about having boyfriends. The driver drove down the road a little and then stopped at a house in Sedona. I guess that was his house. He went in and another man popped up from the back of the truck.

We didn't know all that time that another man was in the back asleep. Anyhow, he leaned over and asked who we were and what we were doing out during the night. He asked us how old we were and we told him. He didn't bother us after that, but when I think back, I realize what a mess we could have been riding in a truck with two men we didn't know and so young. Anyhow, the driver was all right and asked us if we wanted to go to Prescott and we said maybe we better get off in Clarkdale as we had a grandmother who lived there and she wouldn't be angry with us like our father would be when he found out we lost the pass and were hitchhiking. We got off the truck in Clarkdale and walked to our grandmother's house. We knocked on her door and Moda opened the door. She was so happy to see us she said she thought she was dreaming. We crawled into bed with her and stayed with her for a week before we went back to Prescott. We never told our father about the pass being lost, but he found out anyway. Some other people were caught using the pass and my father was questioned about it. He came home and was pretty angry about us not telling him that the pass was lost. Our poor father, he had to put up with what trouble we got into.

Sometimes, in the summertime, the whole family would travel to Flagstaff to see the All-Indian Pow-Wow on the 4th of July. It was those times, that I liked the most – since I was not a reservation Indian, I did not see a lot of other Indians. However, at the Pow-Wow, they were all over the place. Indians came from all over Arizona and other states. I didn't know there were so many different tribes of Indians. How proud they made me feel that there were still a lot of Indians around—that we didn't all get shot down by the cavalry or the cowboys.

One group that made me especially proud was the All-Indian band from the Colorado River Indian Reservation in Parker, Arizona. How straight and tall they were, how good their band music and especially the baton major, who I later learned was named Elmer Gates. He was big and tall and carried himself so proudly! How I loved this band! Little did I know that one day I would marry a member from this tribe and have three sons and one daughter who would also be enrolled members of that tribe.

My oldest sister, Esther, had finished high school in Ash Fork and had gone on to college in Flagstaff at Northern Arizona University and had become a school teacher. She married a Hopi man and they lived in Flagstaff. As she lived in Flagstaff, we would usually gather at her home when it was time for the All-Indian Pow-Wow.

My oldest brother Dan, had married while I was in high school to a Yavapai woman from Ft. McDowell. named Nora Seiber. He became a mailman in Prescott and he and his wife had four sons: Darrell, Byron, Daniel, Jr. and Paul. They also had four daughters: Arlene, Charlene, Terrilee and Doris. Our whole family was very proud of our brother Dan, as were the tribal members, who lived on the Prescott Reservation that one of their own could become hired in the position of a mailman for the city

My brother Aaron had married an Apache/Yavapai woman from Camp Verde named Joanna Gibson. They raised an adopted daughter Sierra and an adopted son named Mark. Aaron became involved in tribal politics and was one of the first tribal members, along with his friend Ted Smith, who got the Yavapai and Apache Nation started. He, and Ted Smith, worked without pay at times and also went to Washington D.C. to lobby for the Nation. Aaron and his friend Ted later got on the Tribal Council as

Chairman or a Council Member at different times. The whole family was very proud of him also. At one point, both my brothers were on the tribal council— that was, of course, before my brother Daniel changed his membership to the Ft. McDowell Reservation. Aaron was elected Chairman several times and was on the Council several times before illness prevented him from working anymore.

My sister Winona had a son while living in Zuni, New Mexico and his name was Walter Eriacho, Jr. She later had a son Michael also, and Ronnie, Leonard and Terry, Jr. Five sons she had and no daughters. She eventually settled in Los Angeles and lived there most of her life where she still lives today.

My sister Deborah had two sons: Kenny Garduno was the eldest. Vincent Gonzales was the youngest in the family. She had two daughters: Deborah, whom we call "Missy" and an infant daughter who died soon after birth. She also settled in Los Angeles and lived there most of her life.

My sister Elividia who later changed her name to Carmen had one daughter who was raised by my brother Aaron, and a son whom it was said died in infancy. There was no proof of this; however and it is not known for sure if he is still alive and living somewhere -- maybe in Silver City, New Mexico. Carmen spent a lot of time in Gallup, New Mexico and Los Angeles, California.

This was my family as I was growing up in Prescott living with my father. One day I was in elementary, then Jr. High and then in Prescott High School. In Junior High I tried very hard at my schoolwork. Math was still difficult but English was easy, also spelling. I became a member of the spelling club because I outlasted everyone in my class in a spelling match. I think I surprised everyone. I was the only dark-skinned person in that club. The teacher was so proud of me and the kids were all nice to me because they knew I was smart. However, the important thing was that I was proud of myself and that was what was important. Even today I like to tell everyone I was the spelling bee champion of Yavapai County. They always wonder where that is. Our spelling club met once a week and prepared for the state finals in Phoenix. Well that day came and we were all taken to Phoenix in private vehicles. We tried our best in the spelling bee, but no one in our club was state champion. At any rate, we were still treated to a trip to Encanto Park in Phoenix where we swam in the pool and enjoyed other activities. After the fun, we were taken home and upon entering Prescott, I asked to be dropped off as we entered the town. The kids in the car and the driver said that they could take me home, but I did not want them to see where I lived so I literally jumped out of the car when it stopped at a red light. They probably knew I didn't live anywhere near there; but they let me go anyway.

In high school, I was often placed on the honor roll. At that time, when a student was making an "A" on a daily basis, they would be placed on a list at the door and that meant that student did not have to take final exams. My name was usually on that list. I studied hard by spending hours after dark sitting near the coal oil lamp studying to make the good grades I needed. And too, after the wood stove went out at night, it would get cold in the house and I knew I had to quit studying and get to bed under piles and piles of blankets. Visitors would usually ask where we were going when we got ready for bed, putting on coats and jackets and extra socks to keep us warm in bed.

One especially wonderful teacher in high school was my history teacher, a white lady named Ms. Mary Ryan. This teacher took special interest in me and was always around to help me. Ms. Ryan even offered me a job after school grading papers and talked to me about going to college and maybe being a teacher like her. This woman gave me faith in myself and I knew she truly cared about me and what happened to me.

There was also a school counselor who got involved with me. The reason she got involved with me was when one day I was in class and the bell rang to change classes. One student whom I had known from grade school (Ruth) got up and left the room leaving her purse lying on her desk. I picked up the purse as I sat right behind her and tried to catch her.

The school crowd separated Ruth from me and not knowing what class Ruth was headed to, I did not know what to do. I felt like leaving the purse in the girls' rest room, but did not want anyone to steal it so I took it to my locker and left it there. Well, during that period, I guess the purse was reported missing and someone probably saw me with the purse and my locker had been searched. The purse was not there when I went back to my locker and I knew they thought I stole the purse. I was called to the girls Counselor, Ms. Julia Rowe, and I explained it to her and she believed me. There was nothing missing from the purse. Ruth never talked to me again, but the Counselor became my best friend. When it came time for graduation day, Ms. Rowe asked me if she could help me in any way. She offered to buy me my graduation dress. She sent me to one of the finer stores in Prescott and told me to select whatever graduation dress I wanted and charge it to her account. I chose a full white dress with a blue ribbon around the waist – what a beautiful dress! I was so grateful to her. What a wonderful person, .just like the history teacher I liked so much. Could someone be wrong about how bad white people are? That's when I started thinking about how our thinking is controlled by what people say and not what we really know about people. Anyhow, these two people were a blessing to me and I have always thought of them with the fondest memories. And too, how I wish I had taken time to go back after high school to tell them "thank you" for their interest in me and their love and caring – maybe they know anyhow, I hope so!

CHAPTER 5
AFTER HIGH SCHOOL GRADUATION

After graduation, I began work that summer in a laundry because my father told me that I could now go to work or go on further with my schooling. He told me that I could not just stay at home and do nothing. I began working in this laundry factory and I hated it. It was hot and certainly did not offer any future possibilities for advancement. Did I really want to fold sheets the rest of my life? No, I did not think so!

Therefore, I made plans to further my education by contacting Mr. Leo Witzleben at the Colorado River Agency in Parker, Arizona, who was an education officer with the Bureau of Indian Affairs. He came to Prescott for a visit with me and scheduled me to start school at the Indian School in Lawrence, Kansas. I enrolled as a Post Graduate in Radio Communications; however the school put me in Business School. My father's wife Annie, who was living with him at that time, took me to Lawrence, Kansas using my fathers' railroad pass. She thought I would be homesick and asked me if I was afraid, but I was not. I was excited to begin a new life in a different state at an Indian School. I had only attended public schools before and now I would be in school with other Indian students. It would be so interesting for me to meet students from all other different tribes from all the other states including Alaska.

Like I said, the school put me, not in Radio Communications as I wanted, but in Business which they thought girls were more likely to need. I did not protest. The school work became boring fast as I had taken all these courses already in high school. I stuck it out, but I was bored. The school did not offer me a challenge.

However, I found excitement in life with the other Indian students such as a good friend from Minnesota who was a Chippewa named Mildred Long. Through the years, I have thought of her often. This girl was friendly and took time to be a friend to me and show me around when I first arrived at the school. Of course, there were a few others too; namely, Grace Eye, (a Sioux from South Dakota), Lucy McCafferty from Alaska, and Lola Patch, Mohave, from Arizona.

I also met several Indian boys with whom I had fun paling around with. One boy who was in my Business classes was Billy Chalake (a Creek Indian) from Oklahoma. He and I were always teasing each other about who came from the best state and who were the best Indians. He was from Oklahoma as most of the students were. He told me that Indians from Arizona were dark skinned and ugly. However, he said I did not look like I was from Arizona. It's a good thing he added that to his statement! We'd argue back and forth and try to get our instructors involved, but they wisely would not get involved. Through the years, I ran into this same guy several times. Once was in Phoenix, Arizona at an Indian basketball tournament and later on in New Mexico where we were both working for the Bureau of Indian Affairs. He was married with several kids and I was too. He was just a nice, friendly person who I enjoyed talking with while at work.

While I was in school at Haskell, my dear Moda passed away. I was given this information by my sister Jane who sent me a letter informing me of the passing of Moda. It seems the family was all upset about her passing that they forget all about me being in school in Kansas and did not bother to let me know or send for me to attend the funeral. Thus, I did not attend her funeral or even know anything about her passing until several weeks later. I felt very badly about this.

At Haskell we had a school newspaper which was the cause of me getting involved with a couple of boys. I had stated to a friend of mine named Velma Stevens, (Apache) that although I was from Arizona, I wanted to go live in Alaska. It was printed in the school paper and a boy from Ketchikan, Alaska named Herbie got in touch with me by a friend he knew named Judy, who was from Kansas and who lived in my dormitory. Although I didn't know her personally, she knew who I was and came to me to tell me that Herbie wanted to take me out. I was unsure of myself and asked her if she was sure. Although she answered in the affirmative, I told her I would sit in the dorm lobby and when he came to pick me up, he could look through the glass windows and tell her if I was the one he wanted to go out with. We did this and she said I was the one. I went out with him a couple of times, but I was shy and probably boring to him so he dropped me like a hot potato so much for wanting to live in Alaska. This did not hurt me badly as I did not choose him so it was all right even though I thought he was a good looking guy. I was not ready for steady dating and really did not think much about holding onto some guy at this stage in my life.

I went with a couple of other boys; although none seriously-- until I met Norman. He was from Ketchikan, Alaska, like Herbie was, and was a little younger than me. He and I were introduced by his friend and began going together. Norman stayed at the school through the summer time and I did too. We both worked at the school. I cleaned the guest rooms for "important" government workers to the school. However, one problem was that my supervisor was a lunatic. She was the head of the Homemaking Department during the regular year; but the way she screamed and hollered at times made it seem like she was not all there. Her husband was a very ill man who would shuffle to her office once in a while whereby she would speak to him very lovingly. At those times, I could scarcely believe that woman could change moods like she did. I began to think that everything I heard about Indian boarding schools were true. They were not good places to be in as a lot of the counselors were mean and uncaring. I often ran into hard times with them because I always stood up for what is right and was not afraid to speak up if the need was there.

A problem came up which caused the dormitory matrons to dislike me even so much more. During the summer, I had roomed with a high school student from Kansas named Berdina and I knew that she was taking my clothes and wearing them. I wrote this in a letter back home and one of my older sisters read it and got angry for me. She wrote a mean letter to the school and got them in trouble so they went after me. They would then come into our room periodically and tear the place apart. They hated me for that. And when I started going with Norman; that was really something for them to hound me about. They'd follow us around, glaring at us and just waited for us to do something wrong. Norman worked somewhere on campus and we went together because he did not go home to Alaska for the summer. We both stayed on campus for the summer and worked.

The next semester we both went back to Haskell. He was nice, and fun to be with when going to school activities. I think that Norman did care a lot for me at that time, but I was not ready for that sort of thing. I had school and a career on my mind.
Considering my future, I made plans to attend the University of Kansas there in Lawrence, Kansas and take my room and board at Haskell Institute. I had a room at Pocohontas Hall at Haskell and my

roommate was a girl from North Dakota – an Arickara Sioux Indian named Yvonne Howard. She was already a sophomore in college as she had previously attended college in North Dakota. We were the only two Native American girls who attended the University and stayed at the Indian School. Yvonne was a sweet girl and very smart. She and I had some good times together. I had a rag doll that I slept with and set up on my bed every day after I made my bed. When Yvonne wanted to tease me, she would grab my doll and run away with it sometimes tossing it down the stairs. We'd wrestle around and always had fun. The semester started out pretty good there, but when I went in for my health test, I supposedly tested positive for tuberculosis and was admitted to the Kansas University Student Health Services Hospital in Lawrence, Kansas. My doctor was Dr. Canuteson, the Director of the Student Health Services. I stayed at the Student Health Services Hospital on campus and attended college from there. When I wrote my father about my problem, he sent my younger sister Jane to come see how I was. She arrived there and I told her I felt fine. Norman came to the hospital to visit me and I introduced her to Norman and tried to get them together as he was younger than me, but Norman was not interested in my sister and he continued to come to the hospital to visit me even after my sister went back to Arizona. My doctor was very concerned about my health problem so he sent me to the University of Kansas Medical Center in Kansas City, Missouri just when I was getting used to my college studies. I felt discouraged then and thought it was no use for me to study. I was lonely and depressed being away from home and around people I did not know. I hated wearing a mask when I was taken to another department like to x-ray. I hated lying in a hospital bed all day and being with all the other tuberculosis people on that floor who coughed and spit up all day. I lost my appetite when they would do this. I did not cough or spit up, but I guess I had a scar on my lungs that the doctor was concerned about. After several weeks, I was dismissed from the hospital and sent back to school where the dormitory matrons at Haskell were extra mean to me. They told me that a person like me could not work in the kitchen anymore. I had formerly been assigned to kitchen detail, washing dishes or serving food. I was the only post graduate student who worked in the kitchen where only high school students were supposed to work. But, when the matrons found out about my health problem, they pointed that fact out that people like me could not do that kind of work. That part was fine with me as I didn't particularly like washing the big pots and pans that I had to clean. I then had to clean the matron's personal quarters which I learned students were not supposed to do. Anyhow, I survived their hatred and continued on with college the best way I could; although I had fallen behind in my studies.

There were about six Native American boys staying at Haskell and going to the University also. Most of these boys were from the Eastern Native American tribes. Yvonne and I did not meet these boys but we saw them catch the bus to the university so we knew they went there also.

Things changed for me while living at Haskell for unlike high school, I had friends and people to spend time having fun with. I got involved in the Indian school activities and having dates and did not spend much time studying. This proved to be very detrimental for me. I did not make the grades I should have and had to take time out. I remember when I had to report to the University Counselor about my grades, he told me that I had to take time out and that anyhow, he didn't find anything in my records to indicate that I might be a candidate for a degree and that I needed to drop out and try something else. This harsh statement from the Counselor hurt me deeply. Did this mean that I was inferior and would never do well? I was disappointed in myself. I had to stay out of college for one semester so I applied for and got a job with the University of Kansas Student Medical Center. The Director at the Medical Center, Dr. Canuteson, who had treated me for my illness was a very kind man so I enjoyed working under his direction. What a wonderful person he was. He boosted my morale as did the other workers there. Mrs. Beamer, the x-ray technician, was especially kind inviting me to her home for dinner sometimes. I felt they all bent over backwards to help me and be kind and protective of me as they knew I had no family close by. Years later, after returning to Arizona, I wrote to Dr.

Canuteson and asked him if I could come back there and work and he wrote back saying that there would always be a position for me there. This made me feel very happy; although I never did go back there.

After working at the Medical Center for half a year, I applied for and got another grant to attend a college in Eastern Arizona. My father did not want me to stay in Kansas where I had no family. I left Kansas and my boyfriend Norman and moved to Thatcher, Arizona where I took up residence in the women's dormitory at Eastern Arizona College. Norman and I wrote letters to each other, but I had started a new life and thought that he would probably forget about me. However, he wrote regularly. I was busy trying to make better grades in this college. This was a Mormon run college. At this college, I was the only Native American girl. There were several Native American guys: This is where I met the man I would soon marry. LeRoy Cromwell Eswonia, was a member of the Colorado River Indian Tribes and a Mohave Indian. He was big and tall and was at college on a football scholarship. As an agricultural student also, he was a member of the Aggie Club and the Rodeo Club at the college. All these things impressed me. I had always loved football; although I did not understand it and rodeo was always interesting to me as was farming. We met and became a twosome at the college.

Even so, I studied in earnest this time with my friends who were, of course, all Mormons. The girls were very pretty, intelligent girls with whose help I made good grades. We'd often get together in our rooms and do group studying. There were about five of us who were really close. Because my friends encouraged me, I joined the (SNEA) Student National Education Association Club and I served as secretary for a while. I also became a member of the Lambda Delta Sigma Club of which they were all members. I attended the Mormon Church services and took religious classes at the school. This, I might add, did not encourage me to change my faith to the Mormon religion. I had been to various churches while growing up, and I had yet to make up my mind which church I would join as an adult.

In the meantime, my relationship with LeRoy, developed more even though I suspected that he drank alcohol, because sometimes he would show up at the girls' dormitory drunk and be rude and obnoxious to me. I was afraid of him at those times and sometimes thought of breaking our relationship -- however, I never did. I did not know at that time that he might have a drinking problem. Although at one time, he did tell me that one of his relatives in Parker, Arizona had told him before he left for college that he would never finish college and shouldn't even bother to go to college because he was nothing but a drunk. This sounded so cruel to me. I could not believe anyone, much less, a close relative could say that to him. He also did not tell me at the beginning of the relationship of the way he had been brought up living with one relative after another and not really having a home and people who loved him, which accounted for and had an enormous bad effect on the life we shared together later on. He was always so unsure of himself and thought no one could ever really love him. I often told him that I had chosen him to be my mate, but he never believed me. Nevertheless, we were a couple in college. LeRoy and one of his best friends, Paul Miller, a Caucasian, from Pennsylvania, were the two biggest guys in school. They both played defensive tackles on the football team. When a great big shadow was seen walking on the campus at night, you knew it had to be either Paul or Leroy.

There wasn't much to do in the little town of Thatcher, but we could walk to the one store in town and have sodas or hamburgers. LeRoy could sit down and eat two hamburgers at one sitting which I had never seen anyone do before. I figured that maybe that's what all the football players did. At one time there was a write up in the Arizona Republic about LeRoy and his football scholarship and how much he weighed and that he was a Native American from Parker, Arizona. I was so proud of him when I saw that article and my father had also seen that article and was just as proud of him too. Sometimes LeRoy and I would study together as we both took Psychology classes. I even helped him cram for his psychology finals which we both passed with flying colors.

Anyhow, after one semester, Norman (the Alaskan boy from Haskell) showed up at the college in Thatcher with an Apache boy whom he met at Haskell. This friend of his was from this area (San Carlos) so he brought Norman with him when they completed their studies in Kansas. LeRoy happened to be there when they arrived and he was very angry. LeRoy got his friend Rudy to back him up and they tried to fight poor Norman. Norman did not want to fight, but he did try to defend himself. Imagine how I felt. I had never had anyone fight over me before and I felt just plain silly. After a few punches at Norman, LeRoy decided to leave and get drunk I suppose. He left and I left with Norman and his friend. It was semester break so I had his friend take me home to Prescott. Norman said that he had finished his course at the school where he was learning to be an auto mechanic and he wanted us to be a couple. Although I cared for Norman, I did not want to settle down with him at that time so I went back to college. LeRoy was angry about Norman but we continued with our relationship. Norman, I guess stayed on in Prescott with my father and I guess he tried to look for work there; but did not have any luck. He met some worthless people and started drinking from what I heard. We did not keep up anymore correspondence. I heard that my older brothers and sisters felt my father should make him leave, but my father did not do that. Norman stayed on in Prescott for several months while I was in college. At some point he did move back to Alaska and I did not hear from him again; although my brother Dan later told me that Norman often wrote to the box number that my father had and would often ask about me. Of course, they told him that LeRoy and I got married soon after we graduated from Eastern Arizona, and that I had children and would not probably consider going back to him. I was told later on that friends of Norman wrote to my brother Dan and told him that I needed to write to him as he had turned into a drunk and needed encouragement to pull himself out of his predicament. My brother Dan did not tell me this until way later on in life.

Anyhow, LeRoy and I both graduated in the year of 1961. We marched down the aisle as partners. My father and his friend, Hubert Arita, from the Prescott Yavapai Reservation came to my graduation. LeRoy did not have any of his relatives come to his graduation which I thought was strange. I thought everyone had a family. We thought of getting married and setting up house even though LeRoy did want to continue college and I did too. Well, we just decided to settle down in Prescott with my father at the old home where I grew up. I soon became pregnant with our first child, LeRoy Eswonia, Jr.

SNEA

RUSSELL, FREIDA
ANN
Prescott, History.

SEATED, left to right are: Paul Provencio, Elaine Davis, Joann Pearson, Cherry Overall, Barbara Hodges and Marjorie Farnsworth. STANDING: Mrs. Holladay, Frieda Russell, Lynn Casey, Jenna Brinkerhoff, Florene Allen, Cheryl Tanner, Frances Cluff, Nancy Burns.

AGGIE CLUB

RODEO CLUB

LEROY C. ESWONIA
Parker
Agriculture

CHAPTER 6
LIFE WITH LEROY

Here begins the story of two Native American college sweethearts who would begin a life together which lasted for the next thirty six years. It is the story of LeRoy and I. LeRoy was a member of the Colorado River Indian Tribes in Parker, Arizona and grew up despite a lot of hardships and not having a family who wanted him. His mother, like mine, had died early on and his father who was an alcoholic did not wish to take care of him so he was moved around to different homes as a child – sometimes just living in the Indian Health Hospital in Parker. There was an old man who loved LeRoy who would go to the hospital and take him out now and then; but I guess they thought he was too old to care for a child and would remove him from that home. That was until he was taken in by a half - sister of his mother. This woman had two daughters of her own and one son. Her husband was a rather important person with a lot of prestige on the reservation. I know that he also had taken in other children needing homes so the family had quite a lot of people living in their household. However, I guess it was all well and good as they were farming people and needed all the help they could get with chores on their farm.

Despite a lot of hardships, LeRoy managed to survive. After finishing high school, in Parker LeRoy joined the United States Marine corps, while only the age of 17. In the Marine Corps, he was attached to the Special Services Division in Camp Pendleton,

Oceanside, California, and in addition to his regular duties in the Marine Corps, he worked in Ordinance in Firearms. He also played football on the Camp Pendleton Marine Corps Team and also was in outstanding rodeo participant—entering such events as bareback, saddle bronc riding, bull riding and sometimes rodeo clown.

When we were living in Prescott with my father, LeRoy got a job working for the Prescott Yavapai Tribe at their tribal-owned sawmill due to the recommendation of a tribal member there, a Richard Mitchell, who was a cousin of mine. Richard knew the Mohave people, as his sister Ruth, had also married a Mohave from the same reservation that LeRoy was from.

From Ft. McDowell, the Government had us move to the Salt River Reservation into a trailer home near Phoenix, and so my Dad and Michael went to live with my brother Aaron in Gila Bend, Arizona where my brother was living at that time. In the summer time, then my father and Michael went to live at my brother Dan's home in Prescott. How our family grew and what our children became later on in life -- especially how my early involvement with Christianity helped me with the struggles of my lifetime is the story of my family.

Let me describe the Mohave tribe as I have already described my people -- the Yavapai people. LeRoy was a Mohave and an enrolled member of the

Colorado River Indian Tribes located in Parker, Arizona. Therefore my four children were all one-half (½) Mohave and they all chose to be enrolled with the Mohave Tribe and with their father's people.

Who were the Mohave? The members of this tribe call themselves the "Aha Macav; their language, like that of the Yavapai is also from the Yuman branch of the Hokan linguistic family, which also includes the languages of such tribes as the Quechan, the Cocopah, Diegueno, Havasupai, Maricopa, Seri, Halchidhoma, Walapai, and Kamia. The Mohave people were called Aha Macav, or "people of the river". The Colorado River was their center of existence. They farmed along the banks of the river. Also from the banks of the river, they made pottery from sedimentary clay and crushed sandstone.

The Mohave traveled throughout the area of San Bernardino County, California. Their name has been preserved in such designations as the Mojave Desert, Mohave Mountains, Mojave River, and Mohave Wash in San Bernardino County. There is also a city named Mojave, and the Fort Mohave Indian Reservation in California (the spelling Mojave and Mohave are essentially interchangeable). There is also an Arizona County named Mohave County.

The Mohave Indians in early times lived in small villages along the Colorado River, extending from its emergence at the Grand Canyon southward as far as

Parker. The most heavily populated area included all of the great Mohave Valley, now a part of California, Nevada, and Arizona

The Yavapai were friends to these Mohave who, it is said, traveled distances of nearly one-hundred miles a day at a steady, easy jogging trot. It has also been said that some of the Mohave men were known to have traveled for as long as four days in the desert without food. The Mohave regularly traveled to trade with other Indians. The Mohave's captives and loot obtained during a journey gave them prestige. The Mohave Indians of San Bernardino County were considered honest and industrious by most of the white men of the Needles area. Compared with the lot of many other Indian tribes of the United States, the Mohave have been very fortunate. Maybe they chose well when they chose to follow the pathway of peace and not war—like many other tribes!.

The Mohave people too are a people of dreams and visions. The dreams, which were called "su'mach", in Mohave were viewed as the source of knowledge. Through "sumach a'hot", a person was given a gift to do one thing better than others, or called upon to receive a gift of knowledge to know how to cure or treat a special kind of illness. A person called to receive such a gift had to go through much fasting and other trials, sometimes not passing the test and remaining like ordinary people. Those who did pass the test were called "sumach a 'ahot" (gifted people).

At death the Mohave used cremation to enter the spirit world. The property and belongings of the deceased are placed on a pyre along with the body, to accompany the spirits. The names of the dead were never again to be spoken. All relatives, however remote, attended the cremation and wept. A person who witnesses a Mohave cremation ceremony can never forget them. To me, who had never attended very much funerals before, thought that the Mohave cremation was unbearably sad. I didn't know how I could take it if I had to go through it for any one of my family.

Well we were living in Prescott for a while. And, LeRoy was working for the Yavapai Tribe for a while, then left me with my father and went to Parker, Arizona where he got a job with the city police as a patrol officer. He lived with his cousin Leona Little and her husband Henry and their daughters Daphne, Kitty and son Merrick and Garrick Scott while living on the Colorado River Reservation in Parker. While LeRoy was working in Parker, Arizona, I gave birth to our firstborn son, whom I named after his father, LeRoy Cromwell Eswonia, Jr. He was born at 1:07 pm on September 29, 1961 at the Community Hospital in Prescott, Arizona. I called LeRoy and asked him what he wanted his son to be named and I could hear his cousin Leona Little and her children in the background all yelling "name him Junior" – so I did. He was little LeRoy Cromwell Eswonia, Jr. with the nickname of Eido.

LeRoy was a tiny baby, so small and I just loved him to pieces. I really believed he was a miracle. I had grown up with so many sisters and my brothers were older that I was not really around any males besides my father and to have my own little baby boy just thrilled me. I lovingly referred to him as my "Eido Bido". I carried him around all the time and would hardly let anyone else hold him. However, my sister "Deborah", who was living in Prescott at the time, would often come to visit and would take him from me and walk away with him. I know she loved him a lot too. Her little boy, Kenny was about six years old and was one of my favorite nephews. He had this cute little baby talk and he talked constantly. Instead of "grandpa" for my father, he would always say "Fampa", which I thought was so cute.

Baby Lee's first visitors were: my sisters, Esther and Jane and my sister-in-law Joanna (my brother Aaron's wife). LeRoy came from Parker the day after his son was born. Also on the next day, I was again visited by my sisters Janie, Deborah and my cousin Agnes (my Uncle Henry's daughter). The baby received gifts from my sister Esther and sister-in-law Joanna plus our good missionary friend Barbara Candee. Barbara was always around to give us spiritual counseling and to assist us in any way that she could.

Baby Lee looked exactly like his dad when he was an infant. My sister's husband at that time, Tommy

Atwood, told him that also when he remarked, "You can never say that isn't your son, because he looks exactly like you!" On the other hand, I thought he also looked exactly like me. Anyhow, he was also a very difficult baby, crying a lot every time he was put down -- maybe it was because he was spoiled. Everyone carried him when I wasn't already holding him. He would not lie down by himself and sleep. Of course, I didn't really want to put him down. I'd often think to myself how a miracle could have happened to me by letting me have such a beautiful baby boy. At times even, I was too stingy to let others carry him. Baby Lee, as we called him at that time, was a fussy baby and didn't sleep all night until he was seven months old -- almost eight months old, by a day. The night he first slept all night was recorded by me as April 27th, 1961. Baby Lee went to sleep at 10:30 p.m. and didn't wake until 7:00 a.m. the next morning. How happy I was when he finally learned how to sleep because now I could get some sleep. I didn't know that taking care of babies was so hard!!

LeRoy being employed by the Parker Police Department as a City Patrolman from September 20, 1961 until October 18, 1961; was living in Parker, Arizona with his relatives. After our first born son LeRoy Jr. was born in Prescott at the Prescott Community Hospital, LeRoy came and took me to Parker where he had been working and we lived with his cousin Leona and Henry Little. The Little's, of course, had their own children – one son and three daughters. The house was full. I was not comfortable because I did not know his family well. His cousin Leona was a quiet person also so we didn't have much to say to each other; however, her husband Henry was outgoing and friendly, as were the children. They all loved LeRoy and did their best to make us feel welcome. From the beginning, I always thought of the eldest girl, Daphne, as the most beautiful Indian girl I had ever seen. She was always friendly and outgoing and she was and always will be my one of my favorite nieces.

And so, we moved back to Prescott to live with my father again. LeRoy did not have many choices for a job in Prescott, although he did apply for a position with the city police, and did not get that job. LeRoy worked at various odd jobs including moving furniture lived with my father, as did my younger sister (Jane) who had her first baby with her, a girl nicknamed "MuMu". Sometimes it would get difficult with too many people all in the same house. However, we lived like this for a while. LeRoy and I lived in the house that was separated from the main house. This was the one with just the bedroom and the small closet area used for a bed sometimes. My sister Jane and I used to call this room "the cool" as the wind from the creek below the hill would blow cool breezes through there in the summertime. But, in the wintertime, it was cold. We had an oil stove which provided heat just around the immediate area of the stove, but did not actually heat up the room. My brother Daniel (who lived in his own place by then with his family) would laugh at LeRoy because he said when he peeked through our window, LeRoy would be sitting in a chair with a robe on reading the evening paper and looking like the room was so nice and warm when it was freezing cold in there.

After a while, we moved back to Parker, Arizona when LeRoy was hired as a Game Ranger at the lower end of the Colorado River Reservation. The Colorado River Indian Tribes provided a house that had just been renovated. It was just inside the southern end of the reservation. He patrolled the reservation and assisted the State of Arizona authorities in the maintenance of tribal and state laws. In addition, he sold permits for hunting on the reservation. I had never lived in a house this fine before. It had air conditioning which froze me at times and I would go sit outside to warm up. LeRoy told me I looked like a lizard sitting outside trying to warm up. I took long walks around the area that bordered our house and often saw ruins where the Mohave people used to live before they moved further north. LeRoy always reminded me not to pick up any pottery or any Indian relics because, being a traditional Indian, he believed the spirits of the deceased owners would still be there. At times when LeRoy was not too busy, he would often go hunting in the brush by the river. There was an old Mohave/Spanish woman named, "Da nu", who lived down there all by herself. She was our nearest and only neighbor. Sometimes she would bring us pies she had made. She would always only speak in

Mohave, which LeRoy was fluent in and understood very well. LeRoy got paid every three weeks as a Game Ranger and sometimes our money would not last. We had very little food and that is the main reason LeRoy hunted a lot. We ate a lot of rabbits and quail and sometimes deer. I learned to like eating the game. It was either that or just go hungry!

During this period also, it seemed like we went to a lot of funerals and I became used to the activities surrounding a Mohave funeral – what was expected of relatives, how to behave and respect the dead and the family. I had never seen funerals of this kind before involving cremation and I felt it was so unbearably sad.

Baby Lee's had his first birthday while we were living in that house in the lower part of the Colorado River Reservation near Ehrenberg, Arizona. My sister Jane and her two children were there at that time visiting us; also Michael (my sister Nona's son). Living there, we felt that we were not getting anywhere. We did not even have enough money to buy food sometimes so we decided to move back to Prescott, Arizona and back with my father.

LEROY CROMWELL ESWONIA, SR. WITH HIS THREE SONS
Upper Right is LeRoy Cromwell Eswonia, Jr. Called: "Eido"
Middle is Sammy Lee Eswonia Called: "Wista"
Wearing Number '11' is Eugene Rico Eswonia Called "Rico" or
"Gene"

Frieda Ann Eswonia

My for-real Indian Doll
My Daughter Sherrilee

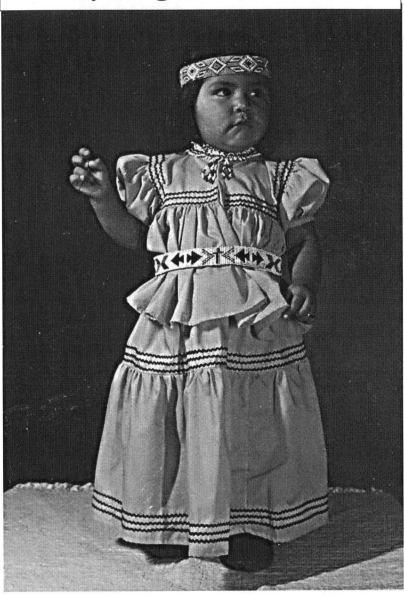

**My only Daughter, My youngest is 'my Baby Girl';
She captured the hearts of all our family and friends.**

152

CHAPTER 7
LEROY AND OUR LIFE

LeRoy went back to work for Southwest Forest Industries in Prescott, Arizona. This time we asked my dad if he would help us buy a car and he agreed. We used my dad's good credit rating and were able to buy a car so LeRoy could drive himself to work. We were grateful though for any help we could get and took my dad on trips when he wanted to go anywhere so he benefited from the car also.

This time while we were living with my dad in Prescott, our second son, Sammy Lee was born on February 25, 1963. I remember the day exactly as I was sitting in the kitchen area with my dad drinking coffee in the morning. When I started having pains, my dad left to call my sister Esther because she had a car to take me to the hospital. She arrived and took me to the hospital because LeRoy was at work. Sammy was born late that afternoon and was a beautiful boy. I was so thrilled to have another son. I believed that my sons were both miracles. I named my second son after my father, Sam. My dad was really pleased about that and told me that my Sammy was a good looking boy. While LeRoy, Jr. had been a fussy baby, not wanting to sleep and always had to be carried, Sammy was willing to eat, sleep and pretty much take care of himself. He was a real good baby. He was also born with his two lower front teeth which amazed a lot of people. He learned to walk at only seven months and I thought it was so

Baby Sammy ▶
Looks so happy and
peaceful doesn't he?

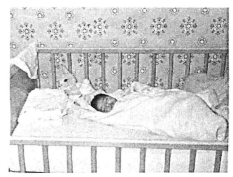

◀   Sammy at 10 months of
age; ready to take on
anything the world had in his
path. As long as mama is not
too far away.

Me; Frieda holding
Sammy with Leroy Jr
(Eido) in front of me; with
his father Leroy Sr. in the
center and my father
Samuel Adams Russell on
the far right. A lot of
memories here.

cute to see him walking around when he was so tiny. As he grew, he always had his older brother to play with and be with – and, he adored his older brother. On the other hand, LeRoy was annoyed at always having a younger brother hanging around. He liked to have his own friends as I guess that is the way with a lot of older children. At any rate, they were very close in age and always had each other to lean on when they needed someone.

After Sammy's birth, we decided we needed our own home so we rented a two-bedroom frame home in Prescott. It was a small home but it had a nice fenced front and back yard. I loved having my own home. My dad would walk over to our house and sit and watch television along with Michael, who lived with him, eat dinner, then walk home. This house was quite a ways from my dad's place, but my dad was used to walking so he would come over whenever he could. Sometimes he would even walk over just to help me and my baby boys go to the doctor's office which was quite a distance from my house. We'd take turns pushing the double stroller because LeRoy used our car to go to work; and I did not know how to drive anyway. I enjoyed these times with my dad because it seemed I got to know my dad better and enjoyed spending time with him. I know he enjoyed watching television as he had never had electricity at his home where he could watch the news instead of just listen to it.

During this period of time, the violent death of our President John F. Kennedy occurred. My dad and

Michael walked over on that fateful day to watch all the news regarding the assassination on television. He told me that he had heard the news on the radio and wanted to watch it on television.

While we were living in Prescott also, we learned of the death of the son of Leona (LeRoy's cousin in Parker) and Henry Little. Merrick was only 15 at that time. We were told that Merrick; was working on his father's land, and driving a tractor, when the tractor overturned and crushed him. He died while being flown to the Phoenix Indian Hospital and the family was driving to Phoenix in their car. What a terrible tragedy that was! Of course, the parents were grief stricken at the loss of their only son. LeRoy, being so close to his cousin felt the loss very deeply too. I had loved the boy too; although I knew him only a short while. Our loss was great!

During the period of time that we lived in Prescott, Arizona, I learned that LeRoy drank alcohol quite a bit more than I knew. There would be times that he would take off to drink with other people and would not return for hours. This was really upsetting to me as we had our little boys and things were going all right. I didn't understand why he had to go drinking. I fussed at him about it and thought seriously about leaving him; because at those times he would get mean and verbally abusive to me. However, I did not have anywhere to go. I had to stick it out. At those times, he told me if I left him he would take my sons away from me, because he knew that I didn't have money.

But time passed and we had Baby Lee's second birthday celebration while we were living in Prescott, Arizona. His birthday party was attended by my sister Esther Scott's kids: Novalene and Gary and my brother Dan Russell's kids: Arlene, Darrel, Byron, Terrilee and "Baby Paul. Also attending was my father Sam and Michael Andler plus Venona Mills, who was living with us at that time. Venona was LeRoy's little cousin—his aunt, Alice Scott's daughter, who was about eight or nine years old at that time.

For every birthday, my children always got a party. I loved giving them parties, because I had never had any as a child. There would be party favors, lots of balloons, and plenty of refreshments for the kids and games. They played games to win prizes and I believe it was a big treat for the Indian children invited, as well as, for my children; because most Indian children were not usually given birthday parties at that time.

This was a good time for me living near my father and my family; but it was not to last. LeRoy was offered a job with the Bureau of Indian Affairs so we left Prescott and moved to Ft. McDowell. We moved into a one-room house which had belonged to my great aunt Maggie Hayes who had since passed on. Maggie's eldest daughter Fannie was living on the Ft.

McDowell Reservation; but was living with other relatives, the Ethel Pilcher Family. She had never been allowed to live on her own and was totally dependent on others to look after her so when her mother died, she was sent to live with Ethel Pilcher in Ft. McDowell. That is what her mother Maggie had done to her by not giving her any freedom at all to choose a husband or go out on her own. And so, Maggie's house was there and we were told that we could live in it while LeRoy worked on that reservation. The house was a one-room house, small but had enough room for a double bed, my son Sammy's crib and a wood stove to cook on. There was an old shed nearby which still contained things which Maggie must have stored away before her passing.

We moved to Ft. McDowell in the summertime and I was heartsick at the terrific heat that we had to endure. We didn't have air conditioning, nor a water cooler or even a fan. I cried a lot wondering what I had got myself into. I did not mind the daytime as much as I did the nights when there was no breeze for comfort. I could not sleep while sweating all night. I would toss and turn all night while wiping sweat from my face and get up the next day in a horrible mood. My dad and Michael slept outside on a bed set under a tamarack tree near the old shed.

LeRoy was the only patrolman on the Ft. McDowell Reservation and his hours were long as he was on call – day and night. As a patrolman, LeRoy was detailed to this reservation which is a 60-mile-square area located near Phoenix, Arizona. The recreation area along the winding Verde River gave him his biggest headache as beer-drinking teen-agers, illegal hunters and picnicking vandals kept him busy. He said that Saturday nights after football games were really rough as there often were so many fights, accidents and disturbances that he would have to radio to the Salt River Reservation for tribal officers to come assist him.

LeRoy was actually assigned to the Salt River Agency but detailed to the Fort McDowell Indian Reservation as a patrol officer. He was responsible for the routine patrol of the Fort McDowell Indian Reservation, and also responsible for the preliminary investigation of all major crimes. He worked closely with the State of Arizona Law Enforcement officers, which included Liquor and Narcotic Control Officers, the Arizona State Highway Patrol and the Maricopa County Sheriff's Officers in maintaining the peace and in the investigation of offenses, both felony and misdemeanor.

Although LeRoy was a big, heavyset man and better-than-average pistol shot, he once got into a big mess when he stopped a car on the reservation to arrest a man for drunk driving. He put the man into the back seat of his patrol car and proceeded to get into the front seat forgetting that he had put his loaded shotgun under the front seat. The man noticed the shotgun and pulled it out threatening to blow off

LeRoy's head. Although LeRoy was scared out of his wits, he calmly persuaded the man to put down the shotgun. He did not let the man know how afraid or upset he was and turned a life threatening situation into a tolerable situation. However, when he got home that evening he told me his life had almost been taken from him and he needed some time off. He took leave and we left for his home reservation in Parker, Arizona for a few days. I'm sure after that situation, that there were many other times that his life was threatened in the long, 26-year period that he worked in law enforcement; but he knew that someone had to do the job and in his opinion, he was the one to do the job and he often stated, "I figure I could have no better job than the one I have and I will always do the best I can." This statement he made was pretty much true for most of his law enforcement career. He was so proud of the job and responsibility he had that he devoted all of his time to his career and doing a job well for the Bureau of Indian Affairs as a law enforcement officer. His own family was slighted at the time, but he did not notice this. However, his drinking was no more a problem at this time. He wanted to create a good impression and did not drink any alcohol.

During this time in Ft. McDowell, my dad was going through some serious mood changes – maybe it was his age or the illnesses affecting him at that time (diabetes, heart, etc.); but he was getting more cranky and unhappy. Maybe, too, it was the fact that he was now dependent on someone else for a home and not independent like he had been all his life. At any rate, I noticed the change in him – LeRoy did not, because he was too busy with his career. My dad would often accuse me of taking some of his things when washing them and giving them to LeRoy instead of back to him. LeRoy didn't need any clothes as he always had more than he could use and instead, -- often gave clothes to my dad as they wore the same size. My dad saying this often made me upset. Reflecting back, I think too, that by moving to Ft. McDowell my dad might have thought he had another chance to get back with his girlfriend and ex-wife, Annie. However, he had seen her only once since moving to Ft. McDowell and she did not appear to need him anymore.--that might have been a big disappointment for him – I don't really know.

At any rate, my younger sister Jane, who had married a black man and who was living in Phoenix at that time, had problems with her husband who often beat on her. One time a neighbor of hers, a Mexican lady, felt sorry for her and brought her and her two kids at that time (Dukie and MuMu) to stay with us for a while in Ft McDowell. Dukie had always been my Dad's favorite along with Michael. My dad would take Michael and Dukie everywhere he went – whether to church or to the field where his Uncle Ed was growing squash and corn. My dad had been given permission from his Uncle Ed to also grow squash and corn and went often to
take care of them. Dukie although very young would walk alongside my dad to the farm which was

quite a distance for a small child. I often told my dad that he should leave Dukie with me at home, but he would get angry and take him anyway. He told me that I didn't do a good job raising kids and that maybe Jane should come and take them back. He told me also that I had a bad record while I was at the Indian school in Lawrence, Kansas where I had a bad time with the dormitory personnel for accusing me of all kinds of things. I think that they were jealous of me going to the university and not taking classes there at the Indian school – maybe they thought I was trying to be better than them and they did not like that. At any rate, my dad saying this really hurt me. A couple of years later however; my dad did apologize for saying those mean things to me and told me he had no right to say those things and that if he could take them back he would.

I did not say anything back to my dad but thinking back on those things; maybe I was jealous that my dad seemed to care more for Dukie and Michael than to my two boys. Uncle Ed's wife, Rena, once told me that she did tell my dad how he was always showing preferential treatment to the other two kids by taking them everywhere with him and never seeming to pay attention to my boys. My dad must have thought about her words later when he apologized to me of the mean things he said to me.

I was very unhappy with the situation. My dad was unhappy and I was unhappy. Although the house had electricity, it was too small. I didn't like cooking on a wood stove. The weather was too hot then turned too cold with no heating or cooling system. Our out house was at least a quarter of a mile away. LeRoy was gone a lot on patrol and I was alone to suffer by myself. I did not drive; but figured I should learn when a cousin of mine started coming over and asking if she could borrow our car because she knew that LeRoy only used his patrol car most of the time. I started taking the car out when LeRoy was gone and drove around the reservation with my two boys. When I first started driving, I ran into a fence surrounding a farm and LeRoy had to pay to get the fence put back up. That was my one big driving mistake as a beginner.

Anyhow, my dad whom I had known always to be kind and uncomplaining before moving to Ft. McDowell, became increasingly mean—maybe the heat got to him too. Then, my Dad just moved away one day to his Uncle Ed's home (which was a short distance away) with Michael. My sister Jane eventually did come to the Ft. McDowell Reservation at one point and took back her kids to move back with the husband who abused her. She had two more boys with this man after she went back to him.

Finally though, the Agency in Salt River provided a house for us at the Ft. McDowell Reservation, a house which had formerly been used as a clinic for Indian Health Service. It was a big house with two bedrooms, a living room, a kitchen, a front and back porch all with a water cooler. I was a lot happier and my dad and Michael moved back in with LeRoy and I.

There was a Presbyterian Church right across the road from our house and we all started going to church there. I began to feel better about everything and I knew I had my faith to lean on and someone to listen to me when things weren't going well. I didn't work but stayed at home with my boys so I had time to practice driving and even tried to learn how to ride a bicycle. I had never had a bicycle as a child and it was a new experience for me.
LeRoy turned three years old, while we were living at the Ft. McDowell Reservation and Sammy Lee was two years old. Michael was around 8 or 9 I guess. It was during that time that my sister Elividia or Carmen as she had changed her name to, passed away in Los Angeles.

Elividia had just visited me in Ft. McDowell a couple of weeks earlier in Ft. McDowell and then had gone back to Los Angeles. She was the sister who was a couple of years older than me, and I believe, one of the prettiest of my sisters. She was a very troubled person though and, it was said, she used drugs and alcohol a lot, -- not to mention her affairs with different men. I loved her though. She stayed with us a few days then went on back to Los Angeles. However, it was not long, when a wire came telling us that she had died.   A few days after that notification a letter came from her telling me that she was expecting and had chosen names for the baby. If it were a boy, it was to be names Patrick, or if a girl, Patricia was to be her name. I wondered if I would be needed to take care of her baby, but I found out that the baby, (a baby girl) had also died.

My dad was upset with how we would have to take care of her burial; but my sister, Esther and my brothers, I guess, took care of her burial and head stone in our home town of Clarkdale. It was not too clear what happened to her; but from little bits of information, I gathered that she had a boyfriend, father of her child, who slammed her head against a wall and she died from the incident. The man was not jailed, but soon died while serving time in jail on another incident. Elividia was the first of my sisters to die – so young and so pretty; but so confused and unhappy!

SALT RIVER RESERVATION

My dad, whom I thought, had got rid of his unhappiness, was dealing with more health problems and was extremely unhappy when he heard that LeRoy was being transferred to the Salt River Reservation. I guess he had talked things over with my brother Aaron and had decided to move to Gila Bend with my brother, his wife Joanna and their daughter Diane. My family then moved to Salt River where we had to move into a small trailer house. It was a two-bedroom trailer, and it was small. We rented this trailer from one of the patrolman from the Salt River Reservation, whose name was Buddy

Gates. I remember Buddy as a quiet, responsible young officer. He had a very pretty wife and two beautiful children – all from the Salt River Reservation. Anyhow, I missed my dad, but he came to visit us when he could. The boys knew him and loved him so much. Sometimes, when he came to visit, he would ask me to rub his back which he said always hurt him. Following my old grandmother's lead, I would rub Vicks or Menthalatum (whatever I had) on his back. I guessed that my dad hated living in Gila Bend, because it was not a place that he knew very well or where our people were from; but I could not do anything to help him there. LeRoy had to go where the Bureau of Indian Affairs sent him and live in the home that they assigned to him.

WORK AT THE PHOENIX INDIAN SCHOOL

In January, 1967, LeRoy was assigned to work on juvenile programs at the Phoenix Indian School under the direct supervision of a Noel Scott, Principal of the Phoenix Indian School, and under the Agency Special Officer of the Salt River Reservation. His duties consisted of the development of juvenile programs for the students. This included the Cadet Training Program which was operated in conjunction with the Salt River Police Department in which five Indian youth were selected and trained at the Scottsdale Police Department. LeRoy was the liaison, coordinator and instructor for the five youths who eventually became employed at various police departments in the Phoenix Area. In addition to this, LeRoy also did counseling and guidance with pre-delinquent youths in the school. LeRoy assisted the Phoenix Indian School in the development of additional juvenile activities for students at the school. This job duty included assisting at baseball, basketball, football and other recreational duties. He was also responsible for the detention, apprehension and handling of all students involved in violations of the law, which included state and federal law. He was also liaison officer for the Maricopa County Detention Home, Phoenix Police Department, Arizona Highway Patrol, and the State Liquor and Narcotics Control Department. What a list of job duties that LeRoy had!

EIDO (LeRoy, Jr.)

My son Eido (LeRoy, Jr.) was four years old, when we were living on the Salt River Reservation near Scottsdale, Arizona. Eido made new friends such as Angie, "Humpy" and Tony Collins who lived nearby and were his first friends. Later on, there was "Bone", and "Hoggy" Hayes. Older friends were Eugene and little Marty Suarez. And too, the boys from Mr. Makil's home and Youth Center took him under their wing and were his friends. His best friend though was Lyle Bighorn, the preacher at the Salt River Presbyterian Church's son. Lyle was a little older at seven, but they played real well together.

LeRoy, Jr. and Sammy Lee first attended 'Headstart' on the Salt River Reservation and then public schools in Mesa, Arizona. It was while living in Salt River that the family came to know Eugene F. Suarez, Sr., who had just been moved to the Phoenix BIA Area as Supervisory BIA Criminal Investigator moving down from the Blackfeet Agency in Browning, Montana and working at the Salt River Agency for 16 months before being promoted to Assistant in the Law and Order Branch in the Phoenix Area Office.

My family became very close to the Suarez Family which consisted of his wife Edna, their three sons; Edna's son from a previous marriage, Eugene's son from a previous marriage and their own son Martin. Along with that family was their friend and housekeeper Lou who met them when Eugene was with the State Department in Santo Domingo. They were all such good people. At that particular time, they were trying to teach Lou (their housekeeper) how to drive and that is also when I was taking lessons to learn how to drive. LeRoy, was busy with his life and did not have time to take me around. I remember Lou's first accident running off the road on the reservation and with good luck – no one got hurt. That reminded me of my first accident at the Ft. McDowell Reservation when I ran off the road and into a fence. No one got hurt, but I had to pay damages to the fence.

While at the Salt River Agency, Mr. Suarez worked with the tribal council to establish the on-reservation youth center; and his work with Indian boys in the Phoenix and Tucson areas was recognized in April 1969 with a Community Service Award by the Dawnbusters Optimist Club. There was a couple who ran the Youth Center, I believe, a Mr. And Mrs. Makil, who were extremely competent and good for the boys. However, they were at an age where they wanted to retire and the Agency was looking for new house parents for the youth center. LeRoy and I were asked to move into the home temporarily and look after the home. We moved in and I took over cooking and cleaning for the boys there. I believe there were about 12 boys living there. I enjoyed taking over that responsibility as the boys were polite and well behaved to me. At that time I only had my two sons, LeRoy and Sammy and the older boys enjoyed watching out for them. There were several trips that we took the youth center boys on and we always had a wonderful time. When new house parents were hired, an Agency house was provided for us on the Agency Grounds.

LeRoy, Jr., turned five years of age, while we were still living on the Salt River Indian Reservation. He was known by now as "Eido". He attended a Head Start program for children living on the Salt River Pima Reservation and he enjoyed going to school there. On April 14, 1967, Eido was in a school play at 7:00 pm. The day care four and five year olds started the program. Then, Eido's class played the three Little Pigs. Eido was the brick seller. I thought that he did a real good job, but that's just a mom's opinion.

For the first grade, Eido went to Franklin School in Mesa, Arizona. He started on September 5, 1967. Eido rode the bus back with his best friend Lyle Bighorn and got home at 3:15. On the second day I took Eido to Lyle's home near the church where he went to catch the bus with Lyle and Arletta Paradise (Lyle's cousin). Somehow it seems that the children who it is expected to be the best and well behaved, because of their parents' position, somehow seemed to be the naughtiest. Well, Lyle was the pastor's son; and Eido was the Juvenile Officer's son; but they were caught throwing rocks at cars and it was an embarrassment to us. However, there were just a few incidents and the two boys were actually very well behaved—not getting into too much mischief!

We attended the Salt River Presbyterian Church where Mr. Bighorn was the pastor. And during the summer months, Eido and Sammy attended vacation bible school at the church. We enjoyed this church and attended the church regularly.

While living on the Salt River Reservation also, my sons LeRoy and Sammy would often tie a cape on their back and run around the Agency pretending they were flying. Thus, LeRoy's boss, Eugene Suarez, Sr., gave them the names "Batman and Robin". Even in later years, Mr. Suarez would ask; "How are Batman and Robin?

Sad to say during this time, my dad who was living in Gila Bend with my brother Aaron also went to Prescott and spent some time living with my brother Daniel and his family. Michael, my nephew was with him for a while and then was sent to his mother's (my sister Winona) for a while. When my dad came to visit me in Salt River sometimes, he would complain about his back hurting and ask me to rub it for him—which I did. Otherwise, he looked to be in pretty good health. However, he contracted cancer in his spine and was hurting pretty bad not long after he complained about back pains. He was still living with my brother Aaron and we would go on trips to visit him there. As the cancer progressed he was taken to the Indian Hospital in Phoenix, Arizona where he was admitted.

All of the family came to visit and it was a lucky thing that at that time, we were living in the empty Youth Center which had five bedrooms and was a very big house. The boys that we had been caring for had been moved to the newly built Youth Center and we were in transition to a home on the Agency. Anyhow, my family all came and stayed at my home while visiting on and off with our dad. We took turns sitting with him in the hospital. At one sitting which we had just finished with my Dad at the Indian Hospital, we were on our way back to Salt River when LeRoy got a call that my dad had just

**Rodeo Cowboy/Clown – LeRoy Cromwell Eswonia, Sr.
Meets – Political High Stepper– Barry Goldwater, Sr.**

passed on. We turned around and went back to the hospital. I was so hurt and even got angry with LeRoy because I had wanted to stay longer and had just left the hospital when my dad passed on. I guess I just needed to lash out at someone and he knew that. I was lucky though that all the family was with me and I could find comfort with my brothers and sisters all together to mourn our dad. My brother Daniel also gave me comforting words to ease my pain when he mentioned to me that I was the one who had taken our dad first and gave him a home when the others did not and I kept him the longest so I should take comfort in that. I was grateful for his words as I had often thought about my dad and wished that things had gone better where I could have had him with me all the time. I cried when I heard that while living with my brother Daniel my Dad had been seen crying and I imagined how he must have felt in his old age, all alone and worried about what he was facing.

Eugene Suarez, Sr., (LeRoy's boss) gave LeRoy all the time he needed to tend to the funeral and he even told LeRoy to take his van, if needed, for the family members and the funeral. We were all devastated at the loss of our father who had been so strong and such a stabilizing force in our lives. We had the funeral in Clarkdale, Arizona and he was buried in the new cemetery in Cottonwood. That was the 20th day of January, 1967, that our father left the family. Our beloved dad had passed away and left us; but I knew he was headed for his home in a better place as he was a strong Christian and lived his life the best way he knew how.

While still living on the Salt River Reservation, "An All-Indian Trade Fair" was scheduled for May 4 through May 7th, 1967. The Pima-Maricopa Community sponsored the National All-Indian Trade Fair. There were members from more than 40 tribes throughout the country including Alaska invited to participate by exhibiting, demonstrating and selling products of their area. The opening day marked dedication of a sports center, first phase of a four-building community complex. The phases were the arts and crafts center, exhibition building and auditorium. The 17-acre community complex upon completion in two years would surround a park for outdoor events. And all the enterprises were under management of the Pima-Maricopa Tribe. The big event for May 5 was to be an *"Evening of Indian Culture" presented by the Institute of American Indian Arts in Santa Fe, New Mexico.*

*On May 6, the program was to include an all-*Indian *field and track meet and an* Indian *Championship Rodeo with Barry Goldwater as Grand Marshal.; sky diving by a nationally known team from Yuma announced by Governor Williams and a stage revue featuring Russell (Big Chief) Moore, a Pima born at Gila Crossing and internationally famous as a trombonist. Will Rogers, Jr. was the master of ceremonies of the show.*

The next day's events were to include a noon Indian-style barbeque and rodeo plus sky diving. The rodeo star included Carol Jean Hamilton. Hamilton, a 12year old Phoenix Trick-Rider and 7th grader who was to perform many of the flashy strap tricks from the most popular hippodrome stand and the daring "Russian Drag", to the "Stroud Layout". The Phoenix Gazette took a couple of photos of Miss Hamilton and the two "Indian Braves" Lyle Bighorn and LeRoy Eswonia, Jr. in an article printed April 19, 1967. How proud we were of that photo in the newspaper, plus LeRoy Sr. standing next to Barry Goldwater in another photo.

What an exciting time for us.!

My third son was born while we were living on the Salt River Reservation. He was named after LeRoy's boss and good, close friend, Eugene F. Suarez, Sr. My third son, Eugene, was born at 10:05 am on Monday, August 12, 1968 at the Good Samaritan Hospital in Phoenix, Arizona. He received gifts from Mr. And Mrs. Suarez, Buddy Gates (a Salt River Tribal Policeman) and his wife, Mrs. Careful (a BIA Employee), Mr. And Mrs. Ralph Pensoneau (also, a BIA Employee) and Mr. and Mrs. Wallace Baker (LeRoy's attorney friend). At birth our son Eugene weighed 8 lbs. and ½ oz. which was more than what my first two sons weighed when they were born – both at around 7 lbs. Again, I was thrilled that I had another son. He was a happy baby and liked to smile a lot. He had beautiful thick, black hair and was always such a joy to me!

I was pregnant with Rico while my dad was still alive and he had told me on one of his visits from Gila Bend with my brother Aaron that if I had a girl she should have my mother's Indian name which was "Dehonja". However, my dad had died before my third son was born. I remembered what he said though and gave that name to my daughter later on when she was born.

After my father's passing, LeRoy was fortunate to be granted finances by the Colorado River Tribes to travel to Springfield, Massachusetts and Hartford, Connecticut for gunsmith training at the Colt and Smith and Wesson Manufacturing plants. He drove our family car and took the whole family with him. We had a chance to see other places along the way -- so it was great! We visited Washington, D.C. and drove down to Cape Cod, Massachusetts. We started on May 7, 1967 and returned to the Salt River Reservation June 8, 1967. We had a very nice time, saw a lot, and returned home tired but happy. We also met some nice people – the Joe Gannon family of Hartford, Connecticut with whom we spent some time. They were sure happy to meet "real" Indians" and see what we really were like – especially their son, who was about 7 years old. I was pregnant with our son, Eugene, when we went on this trip and I actually did not have any problems.

JUVENILE OFFICER AT PARKER, ARIZONA

Although LeRoy, Sr. was doing so well on the Salt River Reservation, it came time again for changes. Our friend Eugene F. Suarez, Sr. was being transferred to the BIA headquarters in Washington, D.C. LeRoy was assigned to a new position and our family would be headed for Parker, Arizona where LeRoy's new assignment was located. Therefore, In August of 1968, a couple of weeks after our son Eugene was born, LeRoy was transferred to work on a new Bureau program as a Juvenile Officer (Rehabilitation and Crime Prevention Program) under the direct supervision of the Agency Special Officer at the Colorado River Reservation in Parker, Arizona. His duties consisted of: The development of a juvenile program and investigation of juvenile offenders who were charged with Federal violations. He made pre-sentence investigation for the use of appropriate courts; presented them to the courts to be used as an aid in sentencing procedure in preparation of rehabilitation programs. In addition, he also assisted the tribal government in developing programs and plans for the juvenile delinquency programs including the promotion of recreational activities and seeking out and developing proper leadership within the community. He also worked with the youthful offender, parents and the courts in planning a rehabilitation program for the offender after they had been released from custody.

In Parker, Arizona, we were given a home on the Agency at the site of the old day school that LeRoy had attended as a child. There were maybe four homes at that site and we had one of them. There were a lot of trees and grass for the boys to play on. I guess it was about five to ten miles from the town of Parker and the BIA Agency and my sons, Eido and Wista, (LeRoy, Jr and Sammy) caught a bus to get to school at LePera Elementary in Poston, Arizona. I had barely learned how to drive and still did not have my license so I was stuck way out there surrounded only by fields of crops with my baby son Rico (Eugene). I didn't go to town or anywhere unless LeRoy was free to take me. I guess this was the beginning of my depression and feelings of worthlessness.

During this time at Parker, we were asked by LeRoy's boss and friend, Eugene F. Suarez, Sr., to take in one of his close friend's son for a while during the summer while LeRoy was working on youth programs. We agreed to take the boy in. The boy was a teenager from Washington, D.C. He flew from back East to Phoenix where we picked him up. He was a tall boy of fifteen (15) with long blonde hair which was just beginning to be the fad at that time. His hair was shoulder length so he was stared at a lot – especially in a reservation town. I thought that he was a nice, polite, quiet boy who fit in nicely with our family. Although coming from a wealthy family, he never complained about our modest home, furniture, car and everything else. He had his own credit card and was told by his parents to pay for his own needs.

When we went out to eat dinner; he told us that his Dad told him that he had to pay for his own dinner. Sometimes, we would take the children involved in LeRoy's programs to different places like, once to California's Knotts Berry Farm, which this boy had never been to before and so he enjoyed it a lot. I remember that one thing he bought for himself was a stuffed red bull. Another time, we went to Phoenix, Arizona with Joel and stayed in a little, worn out motel on Van Buren Street and this boy took off by himself to see the city. When we got back to Parker, Arizona after that visit, he had some marijuana in his possession. We did not know this right off until LeRoy happened to catch Joel in his room smoking the stuff. LeRoy got all excited and called his friend Eugene Suarez, Sr. about what he found out. LeRoy thought the boy should be sent home right away. However, Eugene told him that we should not make a big deal of it and just try to straighten him out as that was really the reason for his being sent there to stay with us for a while. Well, the boy stayed and helped LeRoy with his programs working with kids and got along fine. He was always nice and polite to me and the boys and offered several times to babysit baby Rico while LeRoy and I went to the movies. He liked Native American Food very much – especially tortillas, which he got to eat a lot while working with LeRoy and the boys who were involved in the little league baseball program. This boy, I believe, changed my general outlook on white people a lot also because I always thought all white kids were loud, and not shy. This white boy was not that way at all. I couldn't believe he was so quiet and polite all the time. He became one of the family and later when he left for his home, we missed him very much! People around the reservation often asked us who this boy was and what he was doing with us, but we never told them that he was the son of a well-known columnist who lived in Washington, D.C. Local people would often tell me that LeRoy was riding around the reservation with a blonde woman in his government car (because of the boy's long, blonde hair) and shouldn't I be worried? I knew the truth and it did not bother me. After the boy went home, we received a letter from his mother on September 10, 1969 thanking us for taking him into our home. His parents felt that he seemed to become more grown-up and responsible and that he looked so healthy and happy when he got back home. He also gained weight which they were also happy about. Especially, were they grateful that Joel had a chance to see another part of the country and another kind of lifestyle with another nationality. *I know that he will remember us forever as we will remember the polite, quiet, loveable person that he was and how he changed especially my way of thinking about the white society that I didn't quite trust most of my life.*

As the wife of the Youth worker, I was at every practice and game that the youth scheduled. I sometimes assisted in picking up the youth and taking them home when they needed rides to the Ball Park or Gyms. And, of course, having two sons involved in the games, I had to be there to watch them play. I spent hours on the benches watching my own boys play and assisted my husband with miscellaneous duties. I cherish all those memories of watching my boys play and being involved with them—sometimes helping them practice at home. Eido, the older son, I thought was the greatest pitcher there ever was, a mother's opinion. And Wista, my younger son, was such a helpful and happy boy. He smiled all the time while he was standing out on the field and the coach would yell at him, "Sammy", quit smiling and play ball! Look serious! My baby son, Rico was a good baby and didn't seem to mind all the time we spent at the ball games. He had long, wavy hair which I did not have cut until he was at least two. I would sometimes braid his hair and people would tease me about wanting a baby girl that was why I left his hair long and fixed his hair—maybe I did; but I didn't know that then.

ROSWELL, NEW MEXICO

In September 1970, Leroy was again transferred. This time we were to move to the Roswell Indian Police Academy in Roswell, New Mexico. It was hard for me to leave Parker, Arizona then as I was just getting accustomed to the people and Leroy's job duties plus I was beginning to know a lot of the youth involved in the programs and their parents. However, when the Bureau of Indian Affairs says we have to move—we moved!

The Indian Police Academy was located just outside of Roswell. There, we moved into a house located near the airport where a lot of service men's families lived. Most of the men were gone and there were mostly just women with their children. My boys (Eido and Wista) caught a bus to their school which was a short distance away. Rico was still too young (about 2 years old at that time) so he stayed at home with me.

On March of 1972, Indian law enforcement officers and tribal officials from four states completed a week-long alcohol and drug abuse seminar. The seminar was sponsored by the Bureau of Indian Affairs, Division of Judicial Prevention and Enforcement. It was held under the direction of Leroy, Assistant On-Site Representative of the U.S. Indian Police Academy of the Central BIA Office in Washington, D.C.

Approximately 25 officers from Arizona, Colorado, New Mexico and Missouri participated. Lecturers included officials and experts from New Mexico, Arizona, Washington, D.C. and Missouri.

Identification of the alcoholism problem as well as, the treatment and rehabilitation of problem drinkers was discussed during the early part of the seminar. Emphasis was placed on humane treatment of the offenders. Also discussed were possible alternatives to jail sentences for chronic alcoholics in a search for a workable solution to the problem. The officers and lecturers also discussed identifying the drug problem investigating drug cases, gathering evidence and handling and treating drug offenders.

Another drug and alcohol abuse seminar was also held in Prescott, Arizona including law enforcement officers, social workers and counselors from Indian tribes in Nevada, California and Arizona in attendance. Law enforcement officers from city and county agencies in Arizona were also invited to attend and certificates were presented to those completing the five-day meet. The program was headed by Dr. David Giles of the Southwest Indian Youth Center in Tucson as the group discussed the increased use of drugs among the youth on and off the reservations in the southwest. This seminar was held in February 1972 and attended by law enforcement officers from the BIA and different tribes.

While the family was living in Roswell, New Mexico, I grew to be very depressed because I didn't know anyone and wasn't outgoing enough to make friends easily. I stayed at home with my youngest so I didn't meet anyone. I didn't have enough nerve to drive; although I knew I could if I tried. We had just purchased a new standard pickup before we moved to Roswell and I didn't know that much about standard shifts -- which was just another excuse. Leroy was very busy with his career and was often flying to different area meetings and so forth and I was left alone a lot.

One time though, I remember longing to see one particular movie which was showing in town. I got my boys together and got them into the truck and drove across town to the theater to see the movie. That was one time that I did that and it did take me awhile to get used to the shifting. I probably used first gear all the way to the theater. Later on though, we did buy an automatic car which I used to get around when Leroy was out of town.

However, I was still depressed and began to have anxiety attacks. I could not stand to be in a dark, closed room which meant that I couldn't go to the movies because the darkness scared me. I also could not stand riding in a car because it always felt like the car was going too fast. I once went into a large department store and it felt like the shelves were too high and were going to fall on me. I actually thought that I was going crazy—especially when I felt like I couldn't breathe. I went to several doctors who did not really help me or seem to know anything about my problem. Later on though by reading articles, I found one article in a paper which described my symptoms so that I knew what I was going through and that I wasn't going crazy.

Then it happened that a Native American family moved to Roswell and our family became involved with them real close. They were Indians from Browning, Montana; although the father was a mixed blood of white heritage also—more white than Indian. He had blue eyes as did one of his children.

This, the young daughter had blond hair and blue eyes and did not look Indian at all. This family became our best friends and we spent a lot of time at their house or at our house. We could play cards or all kinds of games until all hours; and, of course, our children had fun playing together. I loved my new-found friend as she was fun, and an outgoing individual. The only bad thing about this relationship was that they drank quite a bit. I also joined in with the group so I wouldn't get left out. I thought that was the only way I would fit in with the rest. One morning, when I went to empty our trash, I had a ton of beer cans to throw out and the trash can was already full to overflowing with beer cans. I thought to myself—boy, we a bunch of drunks! I felt some shame at knowing that what the neighbors probably thought of us. However, I did not stop my new found enjoyment. We never went out to drink, but always stayed at one or the others home.

In Roswell, LeRoy and I became involved with the Cub Scouts as both our sons were in Cub Scouts. They had regular meetings and parades to go to and uniforms to wear. I became an assistant and helped out with the Cub Scouts also. LeRoy and his new found friend both became leaders in the Scouts as his son was also involved in the Cub Scouts.

Later on, when Little League season started in Roswell, my sons both played ball. Eido was one of the pitchers for his team and Wista usually played shortstop. I was proud of my two sons and went to every game spending hours watching both practice and game sessions. Leroy devoted some time to being an Assistant Coach helping out when he could. Well, our son Eido made the All Star Team and brightened our lives.

Well, our friends in December of 1970, had to move. LeRoy's friend who was a police science professor at the Indian Police academy was promoted to Superintendent of Police for Indian Law Enforcement Programs in Macy, Nebraska. It was said that he was the first American Indian Law Enforcement officer in the United States to hold such a high ranking position in the field of law enforcement. Among his new duties would be the development of the first American Indian Model Police Department in the United States, training chiefs of police and to develop new tribal courts, as well as juvenile programs.

LeRoy's friend, an enrolled member of the Blackfeet Tribe of Browning, Montana, was chosen for the post after completion of nation-wide competition. Thus, our close friends, moved to Nebraska just before Christmas of that year, and we were sad to see them go.

Brigham City, Utah – Indian Police Academy 1973

As it were, the Indian Police Academy was then being moved to Brigham City, Utah from Roswell, New Mexico where it was started in 1969 so Leroy was again transferred. Our close friends had already moved the past December and I felt it was just as well that we moved as it was going on two years – probably a little too long to stay in one place! The reason for the move was the fact that it was felt that too many Indian police officers were trained under different concepts and that one of the major goals of the U.S. Indian Police Academy located on the Intermountain School Campus was to provide uniform training for Indian law enforcement personnel. Also, it was felt that the permanent facilities on the Intermountain School Campus was one of the major factors for the move; and too, that the Intermountain location was more centralized to all Indian tribes in the United States than when it was in Roswell, New Mexico. It was also said that the academy would now be closer to the National Indian Training Center which also aids in police science instruction.

LeRoy and I moved around a lot because as he began his employment career with the Bureau of Indian Affairs in law enforcement in 1964, he was required to move where the Bureau needed him to be. Our sons often found themselves in different schools on different reservations and in different states and their schoolwork was often disrupted. When the academy was placed under total Bureau of Indian Affairs control, the policy change also contributed to the move.

In Brigham City, Leroy became the Academy Director. As the Academy Director, he stated that an Indian police officer had to be a "well-rounded" person able to do tasks on the reservation that isn't required in another society's demands—such as, when "old folks" wanted a police officer to bring the mail or gather wood." A police officer on the reservation is sometimes the only person with communications or medical training for at least 150 miles. In that respect, an Indian police officer had to give first aid, deliver a child and be able to do all phases of police work, as well as, investigate crimes, know traffic problems work in youth programs, and help in rehabilitation.

LeRoy said that the Indian Police Academy would receive all kinds of cadets with different educational backgrounds. He had trained men with Bachelor and Masters Degrees and also had one man with only four years of education, but with 12 years of law enforcement experience.

In addition, the academy was there to train men who already had a position with a law enforcement agency and those who were unemployed. The Academy was there also acting like a placement bureau sending graduates to police related fields all over the United States. The Indian Police Academy so far had a total of 650 men who completed the 602-hour course at the academy and it had sent out graduates, not only to Indian Police Departments, but into Non-Indian Law Enforcement field. And too, the Indian Police Academy was open to non-Indians who were working with the Indian people. The course lasted 11 weeks and was geared toward what the Indian police officer had to know. There was training on basic police work plus some advanced law enforcement methods.

When our family first moved to Brigham City, Utah, we first moved into a motel for a while until we could find a place to live. LeRoy was immediately called to service in South Dakota due to another problem relating to the "Wounded Knee" incident of earlier years. He left the family in the motel and left for South Dakota. When he finally returned, we were given 3-bedroom apartment on the Intermountain Campus. It was a nice apartment on the second floor of one of the buildings on campus.

Our family settled in this new area and our sons became involved in activities in their new schools. They both had their pictures in the Box Elder Journal on Thursday, October 4, 1973 for placing in Ford's Punt, Pass, and Kick contest. In a total of 53 contestants both my sons placed—Eido won first place and Wista place second in his age group. How proud we were of our boys!

During the summer, both boys played on the Canyon League in Brigham City and did real well. Both boys made the All Stars team and went on to play in Bountiful, Utah for one full week before they lost out. In this tournament, their team came in second place.

Our boys made us so proud—whatever sport they played, they always did so well!

However, at one of the ball games, our youngest son Rico got injured. It was June 26, 1973. I was watching the games; because I had been asked to keep score. Rico was running around behind the bleachers and I guess someone jumped on top of him. He could not get up and walk and did not tell us what happened. An ambulance was called and he was taken to Cooley Hospital. After an x-ray, it was determined that he had a broken femur—thigh bone. He was placed in the hospital after a cast was put on him. Then was he ever spoiled—not that he wasn't all ready spoiled! All his toys, books, and a television set was brought this room. When he finally got out of the hospital, he had to be carried as he still had on his cast which went all around his waist. He was only four years old at that time and did not weigh very much as he was a slender boy. I carried him most of the time. Of course, he could not begin school with the other children so he had some home schooling until his cast came off. He really wanted to start school too! Sometimes I would take him to the school, carry him so he could see through the windows of his classroom so he could see what was in there. Well finally, he got out of his cast and could go to school like everyone else after being in the cast for over 9 weeks.

Well, a house became available to rent on the campus and we asked for and were given the house.

The house was next to one where a single lady lived by the name of Mrs. Bird. She became a good friend of the family, and would often come over and visit— sometimes eat with the family and we enjoyed her company. This lady was a sweet and wonderful person to have known.

The winters were cold in Brigham City and I didn't get out much. In the summer time though, it was beautiful there! Our sons would go out picking cherries with friends and so we always had a lot of cherries which we loved to eat. An instructor for the academy took the boys to pick cherries one day and they picked too much and ate too much or they got into poison ivy. I don't know which one; but our son Eido came home and started swelling up. His eyes were just slits and he was so badly swollen. We took him to the hospital and he was given a shot for an allergic reaction.

On July 8, 1973, there were 27 graduates of the Indian Police Academy who received their diplomas after eleven weeks of intensive training. The Deputy Assistant Secretary of the Interior, who was guest speaker at the commencement rites, stated in the Intermountain school auditorium told the graduates that they were living proof of the concept of Indian self-improvement. He stated also that the cadets were representing a new era and new chapter in Indian community awareness. He told them also to take pride in the profession.

Frieda Ann Eswonia

EUGENE RICO ESWONIA

Our youngest
◄ son, as an infant;
then as a young
boy: A child with
deep Love, Trust
and Compassion.
He was younger
than his brothers;
in the middle and
he has always
chosen to worry
about stray dogs,
cats and people.

Our middle
son "My
Shadow"
when he
was young;
My phone
sports pal
later on. I
miss his
phone
calls, and
smile.

SAMMY LEE ESWONIA

Our Precious Baby Girl, the
family stabilizer, a constant
source of Strength, Love
and Humor ♥ ☺ ♥

SHERRILEE ANN ESWONIA

LeRoy & me; ▼ with Sherrilee

Leroy Jr.
His early growth from: Infant (below) to toddler (◀) then on to becoming a confident (▶) young man.

Pictured here being held by his Grandma Frieda and Lovingly watched by his Mother Tina. (▼)

BROWNING, MONTANA

From Brigham City, Utah, our family was again asked to move—this time, to Browning, Montana. There, my only daughter, Sherrilee Ann Eswonia was born on a cold, snowy day. My three sons were thrilled at finally having a sister! What I remember most of her birth was the doctor who asked me what I wanted to have. I told him that I wanted a baby girl. He then said to me, "Well, what are you going to do if the baby is a boy—throw it away?" That was an uncalled for statement; but I told him that I had three sons and they all wanted a baby sister.

Browning was a lonely place for me, it was a very small place and again I didn't know anyone until I put in for and received a job with a tribal enterprise which let me go after not too long; as they had run out of finances. I then applied with the Bureau of Indian Affairs and was hired. I worked for a while; but when I had my baby girl, I had to quit and take care of my baby. Sherrilee was only a few months old when LeRoy felt it was time to go home to Parker. He left his government position as Criminal Investigator and applied for a job with his own tribe as Police Commissioner , and he got hired.

Browning, unlike most places we lived, I didn't care for until we moved; then I realized all the good things they had there. They had a 4th of July celebration that beat anything that I had ever seen before. The Indians, mostly Blackfeet, dressed in their beautiful buckskin outfits, faces painted, also their horses and teepees— how fantastic. I thought to myself; these are the "Real" Indians, not the ones you see on television,. They set up a camp and had Indian games and races—how beautiful it was! My youngest son Rico was taking lessons from one of their tribal members on how to do war dancing and he really enjoyed that. We had a tribal member make a buckskin cradleboard which was also beaded for our baby girl which I used a lot. I realize now that there were a lot of things I didn't appreciate until they were gone.

And so we moved again. Our nephew Marty from Los Angeles came to help us move from Montana as he drove the moving van down to Parker where we were going. Our family was back in Parker where LeRoy was once again with his own people. We rented a 3-bedroom home and LeRoy began work there in Parker with the Colorado River Indian Tribes as Police Commissioner.

The two older boys began school there in Parker. Eido was now getting into high school and Wista was right behind him. They both played football on the high school team and were great players. This though began the problem of drinking alcohol for my son Wista. He, and his friends, could easily get the older Indians to buy alcohol for them as they were not old enough to purchase it for themselves. As his drinking continued, he did not get along with the family and was often in trouble for not going to school. The school counselor thought that we should send him to a Reform School; but LeRoy was against that and we just put up with him. Eido was doing great in high school, always behaving and found himself a nice girl to go with. He graduated, along with his girlfriend, and he made plans to go to a military school. This was the Military Academy in Roswell, New Mexico where we had once lived. He left the family and went back to Roswell. After finishing one year, he came home and to his girlfriend. Wista was not in school but managed to get a job with the tribal police department at only 17 years of age. Well, when Eido was set to go back to the military school the next year, he left but came back early when he found out his girlfriend was pregnant. They both went to live with her family who lived across the river on the California side. He looked for a job for a long time and could not find a job. However, he and his girlfriend got married at the Presbyterian Church we went to on the reservation and they made plans for the arrival of their baby who was a little boy whom they named LeRoy, III. As grandparents, my husband and I were thrilled—our first grandchild!

I had put in for a job with the Bureau of Indian Affairs and was working as a Realty Clerk and Recording Secretary for the Colorado River Indian Tribes. My baby girl was taken to the "Cow Palace"—a Day Care run by the Tribes.

Friend from Washington, D.C.'s son, who stayed with us is the blonde against the fence.

Eugene Rico Eswonia High School Wrestling; Rico was well able to hold his ground in all his School Athletics.

Getting out of the protective gear after having won his match and his schoolmate winning his.

My husband Leroy was working for the Tribes but he thought of going back into government service. He was in touch with Eugene Suarez, Sr., who was also a close friend of his, who told him to go back to federal service. LeRoy filled out papers and was selected to a job in Northern Arizona—Flagstaff Area. It seems there was a problem with the Navajo and Hopi which was bringing on concerns so the family moved to Flagstaff. I loved it there. We rented a home on the East side of town. An elementary school was just across the street from our home where our daughter Sherrilee started school. Rico was registered at a Junior High but it seems he spent more time ditching school than going to school; and the reason we found out about this was that our daughter asked me one day: "If Rico's school is that way (pointing one direction) why does he go in the other direction every day?" It was his job to walk his sister to school every day. I was working with Coconino County then. Wista went to high school, but he dropped out because he looked older than the other kids and they were always asking him if he was a teacher. He found a job working for a Security Firm and did very well. We had left Eido in Parker where he was with his wife, and baby. Our stay in Flagstaff was not long; although I loved it there. I practiced a lot on my running and entered several marathons while living there. I drove around in the snow and didn't mind it as Flagstaff was good at cleaning up their streets after a storm. The cold weather did not bother me then as I was young and kept busy. Eido and his little family moved up there with us for a while and he got a job also with the same security firm that Wista was working at. Eido worked there for a while then applied for a police job in Phoenix and got the job. He moved his little family to Phoenix and he was on his way to his own life.

After a year or so, our family returned to Parker to live for a short period. My son Wista got a job with the Tribal Police. However LeRoy was again transferred. When LeRoy was transferred this time, Wista stayed behind to work for the police department. Well, this time, Leroy had been assigned as the Agency Special Officer in Northern California at a place called Hoopa. It was July of 1982 when Leroy was officially transferred to this agency. His job then was to deal with the major problems involved in Fishing Rights on the Hoopa Valley Indian Reservation and the extension at Klamath, California. Major problems consisted of Indians protesting and demonstrating on and off of the Indian reservation due to the State and Federal Regulations that were imposed on the Indian fisherman. Hoopa, is located up in the mountain area, close to Eureka, California. On Leroy's off days, we would go to Eureka to go shopping. Just below the mountain where Hoopa is located, is the small town of Willow Creek where it was reported that the legendary "Big Foot" roamed. There was a giant statue erected of "Big Foot" in that town. Of real beauty in that area, is a stand of giant redwoods. To me, it was like being in a fairy tale place to walk through the stand of redwoods. It made me feel so small to stand underneath those huge trees. There was a river which ran right through the town separating it at one point. In the summer, there would be boat races on that river. It was a beautiful place to have lived – even if only for a short while.

Our family, was given an assigned government house on the agency grounds. In front of the house, was a beautiful big oak tree which had a tire which was tied to one of the branches of the tree. This tire swing was just right for our little daughter Sherrilee to sit in and swing. Strawberries were growing in front of the house and there were cherry trees growing in the back yard—what a wonderful place to live!.

Our son, Rico went to high school there in Hoopa and Sherrilee was in elementary school. Rico was not enthused about school and whether he went to school regularly, we did not know as I was working again for the Bureau of Indian Affairs, Realty department as a realty clerk. Well, Rico met our neighbors' daughter and they started going together. They seemed to get along pretty well.

I do not recall any of the Hoopa Indians using any native language, but they did have cultural dances and native costumes. Most of the activities dealt with the fishing that went on, the salmon and the eel were their choice of food. Once we went to Klamath where they had activities involving tree climbing and

Frieda (Me) ▲ with Granddaughter Lexy   Lexy ▲ a couple years earlier.

More Lexy ▼ the happy baby   Proud Grandpa LeRoy ▼ and Lexy

log rolling which I had never seen before so it was all so very interesting to me! These events I had only heard of before and to actually be there to see these activities was great! The people were friendly and always sharing with us their catch of salmon and other fish—our refrigerator was always full of the fish the people gave us.

Near to Hoopa, lived the Yurok Indians and I would sometimes hear the Hoopa tribal members saying, "Oh those Yurok's! – sounded like they didn't care much for them. I thought about my own tribe and how the Yavapai and Apache were forced to live together by the government and they never did get along just like these two tribes.

On his vacation, our eldest son Eido came up with his family to visit and enjoyed the area too. It was a beautiful place after all. I'm always grateful for the opportunity he had to come up there and spend time with us there; and we had a chance to enjoy our first little grandchild.

At one point Wista got in trouble in Parker and needed to come stay with us in Hoopa. He brought his girlfriend with him to visit us, but she went back to Parker. At any rate, our stay in Hoopa wasn't too long; because Leroy was getting ill. His diabetes problem had worsened – a problem he had since he was 25 years old. He was transferred to Albuquerque, New Mexico and given an office job. This would be his last place of employment with the

Bureau of Indian Affairs. Our family packed up our belongings and got ready to move again.

Albuquerque, New Mexico

And so, our family moved to Albuquerque, New Mexico. LeRoy's office was in downtown Albuquerque; and I got a job working at the Area Office. Our son Wista got a job working with a Security Firm. Rico was only 15 years old and had yet to finish high school. However, we learned that he had gotten his girlfriend pregnant and she would be having his baby soon. She was only a year older than he was. He asked to go up to see her and stayed up there with her while working as a dishwasher and living with friends. He was so young and I missed him, but he was determined to go, so we let him. Several months went by and his girlfriend had a baby boy who was named, "Eugene Everett", after Leroy's father. Rico stayed there in Hoopa with his girl and their baby boy. Her family put on a wedding for them and so we drove from Albuquerque to see the wedding and also the newborn baby boy. They had a beautiful wedding which took place at the Country Club in Willow Creek. Our family went back for the wedding then drove their little family to Monterrey, California where Rico, who had joined the Army, was stationed. He was only 17 when he joined the Army as had been his father LeRoy, Sr. when he joined the Marines.

We left Rico and his wife and baby in Monterrey, California and returned to Albuquerque. Several

Frieda ▲ Introducing: **Eugene Everett Eswonia** "Little Gene". ▲ Son of
"Proud Parents": Eugene Rico and Leigh Ann Eswonia.
Down here we have, "Proud ; Grandpa: LeRoy Cromwell Eswonia, Sr. "
With ▼Lil' Gene

months went by and the couple was not getting along so his wife left and went back to Hoopa and to her family. Rico was then sent to Panama. Rico had volunteered to join the Army, but the United States was also at that time drafting young men so my older son Wista was drafted and left for the army. He went to basic training in the South and was found to have trouble seeing so he was relieved of his command and sent home which meant we had, once again, to deal with him and his drinking problem. He sent for his girlfriend from Arizona and her relatives brought her to Albuquerque because she was pregnant—someone he met while he was a tribal policeman in Parker. She was part French, part Sioux, a beautiful girl. Well, she had her baby and the baby was born on February 14th in Santa Fe, New Mexico—now we were again proud grandparents. The baby was a beautiful little girl. We all settled down together in a 3-bedroom rental house in the West side of Albuquerque which was called "Westgate".

However, Sam and his girl had problems and I believe it was mostly his fault but the girl took the baby and left for Phoenix, Arizona to live with her family. We did not see them for a while; but visited them once where she was living with her sister in Phoenix. Sam came with us to Phoenix and tried to get her to go back to Albuquerque with him, but she did not want to go back. Baby Lexi knew us and clung to us wanting to stay with us; but we left them in Phoenix and headed home.

However, later on, the mother of Lexi came to Albuquerque one day and told us she could not keep the baby and asked us to keep her—which we did. She lived with us and grew up, went to school at a Christian Day Care when I was working and then to Public School—at the same one, Doe had gone to—Carlos Rey Elementary. Her aunt came once and tried to take Lexi, but the baby did not know her and would not go with her. Once we bought an airline ticket for her to take a plane to South Dakota to visit her mother for a week when she was about 10 years old. She would call me every day and say, "Grandma, can you come pick me up" – as if it was just around the corner. Anyhow, I guess the family was driving to California as it was in the summer and so they dropped her off at our house before going on. So Lexi stayed with us and grew up with us.

As the years rolled on, my husband, LeRoy started getting very despondent as he knew his health was going. He had diabetes for quite a while and he started to think of retiring as his health was getting worse. He took one trip to the Zuni Pueblo southwest of Albuquerque where the tribe had asked him to come and try out to be the judge in their court. While being interviewed, LeRoy fainted and was taken to a hospital where they determined that he was a pretty sick man. The Bureau of Indian Affairs kept a close eye on him as he had taken several hospital stays due to his bad health. They then suggested to him that he needed to retire. A retirement party was held for him and he was barely able to make it there, because he was having problems with his legs. The doctors called it, "Neuropathy" resulting from his diabetes (a nerve problem) which was untreatable. LeRoy could not see very well, hear very well or walk very well. Everything in his body seemed to be affected by his diabetes!

LeRoy's Illness Worsens

LeRoy thought about our family needing a home of our own and so he bought a double-wide trailer home with his retirement money. The trailer home was brand new and so beautiful! We had it set up in a mobile home park on the west side of Albuquerque at the site of 9-mile hill. At that time, the park was well run and had nice lawns and a club house next to a big pool. We loved it there. There was my son Rico, his girlfriend Monica and baby Sally Jo, my son Sam and his little Girl Lexi, and our daughter Doe plus LeRoy and I.

I was employed with a law firm at that time which dealt with water rights for Indians among other cases. There were three attorneys in that firm who handled other cases. It was an interesting job and I treasure all that I learned in that firm. During that period Leroy became more and more ill. Family from Arizona came to see him and spend time with him. Leroy's kidneys had failed and he was given a bag to use which they trained me to put on him and replace every day. I was his home nurse, as well as, the whole family. We all took turns taking care of him as he was in a wheelchair now and unable to walk. We set his wheelchair in the living room, on front of the television set. Sometimes though to relieve boredom he would use a spoon and tap on the card table which he ate his meals on. My granddaughter, Sally Jo, and her mom were staying with us then. Sally Jo, who was around two years old, loved to sit under the card table. When LeRoy started tapping with his spoon, Sally Jo would answer his taps with a spoon also. They would go on like this playing some kind of tune known only to them. When Sally Jo's mother found a job at a hospital not far from our home, there was a question, on who would watch the baby Sally Jo. LeRoy said, "Leave her with me, I can watch her"; we knew he wasn't able to watch her so we all pitched in and took care of her. I loved having her as my kids were all pretty much grown now. I'd take her for walks in the park, but she could get away from me pretty fast on her little chubby legs. I would push her in the swings, let her play on the slide and then take her home. I finally ended up buying her a wagon so she could sit in there and not get away from me on the walk to and from the park. I also bought her a little red peddle car—much like the one Lexi had when she was that age. One thing she really enjoyed though was taking baths with me. In that trailer house we lived in was a great big oval shaped bathtub and the two of us would take bubble baths together. She would follow me around say "bass gamma", bass". Which, of course, meant bath, grandma bath? After the bath, I would towel myself then take her out of the tub and, as soon as she got out, she would run from me all naked through the trailer house hallway. Her mother would have to chase her and get her clothes on her. I loved those times with her and my heart broke when her mother left my son and took the baby with her back to her mother's home in Santo Domingo.

The family did not see the little girl again for years; because of the breakup of her mother and my son Rico. We did try to visit her at her mother's home in Santo Domingo once. I, my daughter Doe, and Lexi drove up there and visited for a while when the girl's grandfather became upset at us being there. He called the tribal police who came and ordered us off of their property. I was devastated but could do nothing. We left and it was years before we could see the little girl again!

One day a call came from Monica, Sally Jo's mother who said her little girl wanted to see us—somehow she had remembered us and asked to see us! We drove to a grocery store and Monica met us there with Sally Jo. I cried when she came out of their car—a little girl now about six or seven years old. She was quiet trying to remember us. We all gave her hugs and asked if she could come see us again; but we didn't see her again for a long, long time and time marched on leaving us all a little older.

One day at a hospital checkup, Leroy was told by the doctors that his condition had worsened to the place where he needed to be put on a dialysis machine during the night time hours. They would bring the machine and set it up in our bedroom. LeRoy was very strong about refusing the machine. He said that he would not use the machine even though I told him that he had to use it for his own good. That was on a weekend that I gave him that news and I was expecting the machine to arrive that weekend so he could begin using it on the following Monday.

Well, that weekend, I brought home some Kentucky fried chicken for the family and, as usual, we set up the card table for LeRoy at the couch where he always sat to eat and watch television. The rest of us sat at the table and were preparing to do so when LeRoy said, "I want to sit and eat with the family at the table this evening." We set him up at the table with us—which, unknown to us, was to be his last meal. Later on that evening, he kept on being anxious and wanting to go to the bathroom frequently; but he really did not need to go. Around 11:00 p.m., when everyone was already asleep, he woke me up to say he wanted to go to the bathroom again. I was the only one awake and could not lift him from the couch as he was not helping to lift himself off of the couch. I told him that I could not lift him and he started kind of jumping on the couch to see if he could stand up, which still did not help. I woke up my son Rico and asked him to help me get his dad to the bathroom and he got up to help me.

We took him to the bathroom and had a hard time lifting him to the toilet seat. LeRoy had gained so much weight and really was heavy! After he had really not done anything, we tried to lift him to the wheel chair to take him back to the couch; but we could not lift him again! He was too heavy for us! We decided to let him lie on the floor as it was all carpeted and my bed was close by him. We covered him up with a blanket. He lay on the floor and just a few steps away from where my bed was—but sometime during the night, I heard him move and his foot banged against the cabinet in the bathroom. I looked up, but he seemed to be all right so I went back to sleep. He didn't make any noise of discomfort. In the morning, I got up and got his bag ready to drain, got his medicines ready, and then looked at him. His eyes were wide open. I told him that it was time for the bag change, but he did not respond. I kneeled and looked closer and then realized that he did not hear me. I then went to my son Rico's bedroom and woke him up telling him that his dad would not wake up. Rico came with me, kneeled down with his dad then headed straight for the phone. I kneeled down again and it hit me that LeRoy was gone. I cried and cried which woke up Lexi. I called my daughter who was at that time, living with her boyfriend in Rio Rancho. She came right away. Rico called our Pastor David Ashmore from our Church and he came over very quickly. The coroner came and then the mortuary people came and took LeRoy away. It was a devastating time for me and the family! The date was August 12, 1994—

my son Rico's birthday; but his birthday was forgotten in this tragedy.

Funeral arrangements were made by someone I don't know whether it was my oldest son Eido or who, I don't know. Our Pastor, David Ashmore and his wife flew with us from Albuquerque to Phoenix where he rented a car and drove us to Parker where the funeral took place. My son, Rico and Monica drove to Parker in their car. It was a very sad day for the family! There was a church service at the reservation Presbyterian Church; then, there was the traditional wake with Mohave gourd singers. At day break, Leroy was taken to the town cemetery because he had not wanted to be cremated the traditional Mohave way.

Talking to me about LeRoy earlier, the Pastor had said to me that he was wondering why it was that LeRoy had been so anxious that evening before he died and had wanted to constantly move around in the house. He said, "I thought LeRoy was a Christian and would be calm and ready to go to his final resting place, but hearing that he was restless, I wonder if he was a Christian." Later on, while waiting for the plane to go to Phoenix, he, the pastor, became impatient waiting to leave—pacing back and forth in the airport and it was then that he realized that must have been why LeRoy was so impatient waiting to go also-he was ready to leave and thus became impatient! Well, anyhow after the funeral in Parker, we all left together for our home in

Albuquerque leaving our LeRoy behind—what a sad time!

So it was, that life in Albuquerque went on without LeRoy, my husband and head of our family. I had my two sons, my daughter and my granddaughter. Life became a struggle then, as my two sons had their alcohol addiction problem which was unbearable to me and my girls. When my sons got drunk and mean; it was very hard for me to handle them all by myself. Sometimes, I would just take the girls and go over to a church member's house to get them away from the boys. My daughter later moved in with her boyfriend so she was ok. I began to feel life was being very unfair to me. Although I had been working at the law firm, my boss let me go right after my husband died. Why, this happened I do not know—maybe he thought I would not do a good job grieving over my husband. So, I kept on struggling with my sons drinking problems and also trying to raise my granddaughter who was turning into a very unruly child. She was outgoing and made friends easily and would spend a lot of time away from home. I struggled with my family and found it was not an easy job to take care of a family by myself.

Time passed though and my granddaughter was growing into a beautiful girl and entered into high school. My daughter had already graduated and was working. The boys worked when they could. Anyhow, Lexi's friends were not the type that I approved of, but I could not monitor her actions all the time as I was again working. I found out later that she had not spent a lot of time in school, but would cut classes and spend time with her friends.

The family was still living in the trailer home that LeRoy had purchased after he retired. It was once so beautiful but seemed to wear out very quickly. The living room floor had to be fixed. The master bedroom's bathroom had to be fixed. The roof seemed to be coming apart. We never seemed to have enough money to last through the month. I barely made expenses every month and got behind on my rent at one point when I called my brothers, (Aaron and Daniel, in Arizona and asked for help. They got together and sent me my rent money which was so good of them! But then, they were always good to their sisters—helping out whenever they were asked. They took over the job of being father and mother to us sisters. It seemed to be quite a while before LeRoy's money for annuity came in and that helped our family out tremendously.

I eventually got another job with another law firm doing civil cases, family law and immigration cases. There were three attorneys there in this law firm— two older men and one young attorney. There the office help consisted of me and two other ladies. I found it a nice place to work! The staff (all Anglo) were cordial and accepted me wholeheartedly!

During that first year after my husband's death, I remained with the Foursquare Church which the family had attended before LeRoy's death. We knew the pastor, who went with us to the funeral in Parker, Arizona and his wife plus all of the other parishioners so we felt comfortable there. The people there were our support at a time when we, especially I, needed support and comfort!

▲ A "Crew of Characters"; all Russell : With our Cousin Bobby and I; sandwiched between my "Brothers Aaron and Daniel.

◄ Over here is My Brother Daniel, whom I miss so much; in part because he would call me almost daily just to talk and laugh; his death left "A Void" in our family. We certainly all miss "Dan".

SAMMY LEE ESWONIA
My middle son, my shadow, my confidant; He talked to me and though he had been sick for some time; his untimely death tore me apart and at times I still miss receiving his calls.

EUGENE RICO ESWONIA

My youngest son: Enlisted at the age of 17 and the turmoil that ensued, which cost him in ways I cannot possibly understand. A precious child, compassionate teenager, super sensitive adult and my Loving Son.

A New Man in my Life.
Pictured with me; in Flagstaff at the Arizona American Indian Living Treasure Award Presentation in October 2007

Let me introduce you to my husband "Dale Earl Gohr".
Dale and I met while attending the same Church in Albuquerque, New Mexico; I'm not sure exactly when but I think it was in 1993; although we did not actually get acquainted until early 1996 just before he went back to driving 'coast to coast'. Then in September 1997 we got married on the Colorado River in Laughlin, Nevada. Now we live in Clarkdale, Arizona and we each cherish the other ones company and a beautiful marriage.

CHAPTER 8
A NEW MAN IN MY LIFE

I was alone but I figured I could handle it alone, at first, without a husband. However, there were things that had to be done that just weren't meant for a woman to take care of – they were a man's job. Then it happened that I met a man who had started coming to our church—,who I thought, at first, was just a bachelor. This man began coming to church regularly and I heard that he had moved in with one of the church families. They would all come to church and he would sit with them holding their youngest child on his lap. Our pastor thought that this man was a match for me and often encouraged me to invite him to dinner. I resisted at first until my daughter and granddaughter said I should invite him also. Due to my girls urging, I called him one evening at the home of the family that he was living with and the girls there told me that he was out taking his ex-wife to dinner. This was news for me as I did not know that he was still going out with his ex-wife. They were divorced, but he met her every now and then, I guess to help her out with expenses. However, at times he would invite me to his office holiday dinner so I finally agreed and went with him. It was a nice dinner and I met some of the people that he worked with. After that, we started going out every now and then. My girls were all right with it; but my sons did not like the idea of me going out with another man.

When we started going out regularly, this man, whose name was Dale, went out and got a trucking job, driving the big semi-trucks from coast to coast to earn more money. We had invited him to move into our trailer house and he had moved into one of the bedrooms which happened to be empty because my son Rico had moved to his girlfriend's place and my son, Wista was living elsewhere also. My daughter Doe had moved to her boyfriend's house and there was only my granddaughter, Lexi left at home. Dale put his stuff into Doe's bedroom; but then was out on the highways, most of the time, driving from coast to coast. The hill that we lived on (9-mile hill) had a truck stop so he would often stop there on his way from one coast to the other. Dale accepted my family and I thought it was ok since he didn't seem to have any family of his own and I had plenty!

One day, Dale called and told me that he would be stopping by the next day on his way to the west coast and asked me to go with him. He said we could stop over at Laughlin and get married and then go on to Los Angeles where he would drop his truck load off, and that we could visit my sister Nona and Dave. I thought that he was a very nice, Christian man and my answer was, "yes". My daughter who had wanted me to go out with him at first, had a change of heart and did not want me to go out with him. I didn't know why except that maybe he was taking my attention from my family to include him. Ricky and Sam, my two younger sons who were heavily into drinking did not want him around and were rude to him. My granddaughter got along with him and didn't mind him at all. Anyway, I told them all that I was taking a trip with Dale and left my granddaughter in Doe's care. Dale and I had a nice trip to Laughlin in his semi-truck and got married on a Riverboat while on the Colorado River. We stayed one night there and went on to Los Angeles. On our way back, Dale dropped me off in Albuquerque and went on to the east coast and that is how we began our life together!

My eldest son, Eido came for one visit in Albuquerque , which was to be his last visit. He had some problems with his wife and apparently had a girlfriend whose home he had moved to leaving his family behind. The new woman was a Criminal Defense Attorney who had her own law firm in Phoenix. Eido wanted to leave his wife, but she would not let him get the divorce he wanted. Anyhow, he came to see us bringing the kids to visit and it was so nice to have him there. He got along so well with my husband Dale and we had such a great time. As it was near the Fourth of July, we had bought some fireworks and we all went out to an open area in the desert night so the guys could set off the fireworks. Little did I know then that this would be the last time I would see my eldest son alive! While he was there with us in Albuquerque, he slept on the couch and I got up early and was sitting next to the couch and I remember so well his beautiful thick, black hair. After he went back to

Phoenix, he would call me sometimes and ask me how to cook certain things as he was living with his girlfriend and wanted to do more cooking on his own. Still working with the Phoenix Police Department, he had been promoted to a Detective and was also working with the Drug Enforcement Agency. He had met his girlfriend while working there as she was one of the attorneys who worked with the Phoenix City Police Department.

Several unusual things happened after Eido left Albuquerque after his visit which, I believe, were signs trying to tell me of his coming death. I did not pay any attention at that time and did not heed the warnings. One such event happened one night after I had gone to bed. Usually, I went to bed after the late news. I had been asleep when the phone rang and it was my son Wista. He usually called me after a night of drinking for me to pick him up in downtown Albuquerque. I got into the car and began my descent into town from our trailer home on nine-mile hill. All of a sudden, I see millions of stars falling. They were so close that I felt that they were going to hit my car. In fact, I felt something hit the car on the right side and I thought to myself, "Are the stars really falling or is someone throwing rocks down from the hill?" When I felt something hit the car, I asked myself how I was going to get the car fixed as that rock probably made a big dent. I drove on down the hill and found Wista right on Central waiting for me as he said he would and I picked him up. When he was going to get in the car, I asked him if there was a big dent on that side of the car so he looked and said there was nothing. I thought that was strange. I got home and figured maybe there were people throwing rocks on the hill so I called the Albuquerque Police and told them that rocks were being thrown at cars and they said they would check. I couldn't figure out why this strange thing happened—maybe it was something just for me as later on that month, I had bad news concerning my son Eido.

I was up early one morning drinking my coffee and had my breakfast ready to eat when the phone rang. I answered it and it was from my daughter-in-law, Eido's wife, who said, "LeRoy is dead." It didn't quite register with me at first and then I began to cry. I couldn't eat my breakfast. Sam knew that I had been talking to Eido's wife so he called her back and learned that his brother Eido had died in an accident while in Jamaica where he had gone on vacation with his girlfriend. I called Rico who was then living with his girlfriend Susan and they came over. I then called Doe and she came over with her boyfriend Chris. We all sat around crying and trying to decide what to do. I asked Doe to pray for Eido with me and we knelt down and prayed for his salvation. Like I said before, I do not know who made all the funeral plans as I could not think clearly to do anything. Anyhow, plans were made and we had the funeral at Parker. Only three years after my husband Leroy died, now our son's death. What a loss for me and my family!

My husband, Dale, was on a road trip at that time of Eido's death when he called me from Grants and found out that my son Eido had passed away. He said he would be home as soon as possible. He went on to Moriarity and relayed what had happened and got time off for the funeral and came home to console the family. He loved Eido and got along so well with him, I know we would have had great times all together if we had been given the chance. While at home waiting for the funeral, Dale wrote a beautiful poem about Eido and this was recited at the funeral service. The following is the poem that Dale wrote about Eido:

EIDO

I know no meaning for this name
I only know the man
Who means so very much to me
My step-son, brother, friend.

His smile, oh, so contagious
His warmth was felt by all
His strength seemed so outrageous
You'd think he couldn't fall

His children are his legacy
They're worth much more than gold
They share his strength, they share his love
A love that won't grow cold

There are so many "men" today
Whose love is like the sand
It blows around with every wind

It dares not take a stand.

There are so many people here
So busy with their lives
They cannot see their childrens' needs
Won't wipe tears from their eyes

In Eido, strength was through and through
Himself—not his goal or plan
He raised his children straight and true
Life shows he took a stand.

He left us now to carry on. Let's learn from what he's done
We have not the final say, with God, his race is won.
No matter how you slice it friend, Jesus is the one
In whom this fragile life exists, from where good things have
come.

His children are his legacy
They're worth much more than gold
They share his strength, they share his love,
A love that won't grow cold.
Dale

While we were in Phoenix, another weird thing happened at the funeral home that I can recall. This phenomenon was also seen by Lexi and Doe who stood next to me as we viewed the body of Eido. The body seemed to be taking deep breaths as if he were still alive and trying to breathe. I moved back to see if there was something under the casket which was making the body do that deep breathing.   I remember later that Lexi and Doe also told me later that they also saw that happen. Months later, Dale, my new husband, who had returned from one of his road trips, told me that he had been praying for Eido to come to life briefly in order to accept Jesus as his savior. Therefore, I believe, in my heart; that was the reason for what happened. What a tragedy; but the family moved on without Eido who we had all come to lean on as the head of our family. My two other sons worked as much as they could until their drinking problems got them in trouble. I had a hard time trying to handle the two or just plain did not know how.

As luck would have it, my son Wista then got in big trouble. I, who never got sick, did get sick and that is when everything went bad. One evening, I just could not handle pain in my stomach and asked Wista to take me to the hospital. It turns out that I had a gall bladder problem and they kept me in the hospital for surgery. That was at the Indian Hospital in Albuquerque. This was the first time that I did not spend my night at home. My son, Wista, with his drinking, got into so much trouble that he was taken to jail. Our new pastor from the Native American Assembly of God Church, Pastor William Fragua, helped all he could, by standing by me when they took my son away. My heart was broken! Pastor Fragua and his wife were such a blessing!

My new husband, Dale, was on the road a lot and I had to spend a lot of time alone in the trailer home. What a lonely, sad time for me! Lexi was in high school and hanging out with her not-so-good friends and I just could not do anything with her.

As time went on, the family settled down to a routine until my brother, Aaron, from Clarkdale called and told me that the lot that I had chosen for my home in Clarkdale was being questioned by the Chairman. He was wondering why the lot was not being used by me and my family and was saying that they should give the lot to someone else. Aaron told me to at least put up something on the lot—like a fence or anything so I could began considering moving to Clarkdale. I wrote to the Yavapai and Apache Nation and told them that although I had a trailer house that I was living in at Albuquerque; it had become run down in years and was not suitable to move to Clarkdale to put on my lot. I asked for a house and they miraculously agreed to set up a three-bedroom home on my lot. The Nation began work on the house; and eventually, it was available for me to move into. I had second thoughts about leaving Albuquerque and my daughter and sons, plus all my grandchildren that I loved; however the thought that I would probably get taken care of by my Nation and not be a burden to my children in my approaching aging years gave me the decision to move. My husband Dale was all for the move and thanks to his knowledge of packing, the moving van we rented was securely packed and everything we wanted to move was ready to go.

I drove my little green car, a Geo Prism, also packed with our belongings and followed Dale who was driving the moving van. We stopped once at the

Giant Station outside of Gallup, New Mexico and then drove on to Arizona. We had our walkie talkies to keep in touch with each other on the drive. Lexi, being a teen ager now had dreaded moving away from her friends and had run off before we left Albuquerque. Wista was not there. Rico was with his girlfriend and working at that time for the City of Albuquerque. Doe was most unhappy at us moving; but she was with Chris. And so, we moved! We arrived in Clarkdale, at our house and began unpacking late in the afternoon. My brother Aaron and his wife, Joanna, came over to help us move our stuff into the house. That evening, in July, 2001, Dale and I slept in our new house on a mattress on the floor of our bedroom. What a different life we would begin there in the Indian Community of Clarkdale, Arizona!

So, our new life began at our new home on the Reservation at a brand new house which was next to my brother Aaron's house on a hill just before the road which went down to the main reservation. Since Dale was still driving trucks, he left me to set up the house. I sent for Doe and she came over to stay with me for a while to help out. Dale spent a little more time on that cross country driving then applied at the Clarkdale Cement Plant to drive for them. He was hired almost immediately and worked for them while I stayed home for a while. However, I had applied at the Nation's Personnel Office for several jobs and soon received a letter not long after I applied. I got an interview for the tribal court. I was happy for the chance to work again even though I was already getting my social security having retired in Albuquerque. Soon after the interview, I was hired as a Court Clerk. The supervisor who hired me and a lot of the other employees around did not know me and the fact that I was from the "Russell Family" of Clarkdale, as I had kept my first husband's last name "Eswonia"—simply because it is a beautiful Indian name. My husband Dale's name is "Gohr" as he is from German lineage and that name did not fit me—being a full-blood Indian. Anyhow, my supervisor, was a young woman of Apache heritage. She later found out that I was related to the Chairman, who had just been elected, and who was my brother Aaron. She, hearing rumors that the Chairman might be related to me, came right out and asked me one day if I was related to him and I answered that he was my brother. That threw her way off, as apparently, her family did not like the Russell Family. She then began a campaign to make my life working in the court as miserable as she could make it.

My granddaughter, Lexi, had since moved back with us in Clarkdale and was living with us and attending high school. Lexi used my car during the day and would pick me up in the evening at the court. Thus, Lexi became acquainted with my supervisor and they became good friends. Then behind my back, the two conspired to get Lexi back to New Mexico because Lexi found out she did not like living in Clarkdale—it was too much a "one horse town" for her. One day, the supervisor took a day off from work, drove to my house in Clarkdale and helped Lexi pack her things, took her to her home in Middle Verde and let her stay at her house for several days before she had her uncle drive Lexi back to Albuquerque. I had gone to work and went home that one day to find Lexi's room in a mess! She had gone through all her things and what she did not want, she just threw on the floor. Lexi was gone! I didn't know what happened—she was not yet old enough to be on her own. I called the tribal police and reported her as a run-away! My supervisor never gave a hint that she knew what happened to her; yet she worked by my side all that time. She must have known how I felt—worried and devastated. I didn't know what had happened to her. For months I waited to have Lexi come back or even to call and let me know that she was all right. I imagined all kinds of scary things might have happened to her—you could not imagine the heartbreak I went through.

Well, over half a year passed, when I finally had a clue as to what happened. My daughter Doe in Albuquerque happened to be on her computer one night and saw something on line which was written by Lexi. She called me right away and let me know. I was relieved, but also saddened at what she had put me through! I guess that Doe had got in touch with her and Lexi had told her that she wanted to come home. We sent her airfare and picked her up in Phoenix; but she appeared to either be intoxicated or on drugs,--not talking much, just sleeping all the way to Clarkdale.

When she got around to it, Lexi finally told me who had helped her run away and I was shocked! It was my supervisor. Why did my supervisor do this to me—she didn't even know me enough to hate me like that. I went to the tribal police and reported to them what was done and this supervisor had to quit her job and was just lucky she did not get thrown in jail. Of course that is how the tribal government operates, they do not punish anyone like they should be punished. This supervisor got away with "kidnapping", and crossing state lines with a juvenile; but she was never punished as she should have been. The tribal court set up mediation with me and their family. She quit her job as Chief Deputy Clerk and that was all that was done.

I quit my job at the tribal court and began looking for another job. I had a cousin who offered to help me by hiring me at Yavapai Culture as an Assistant Language Teacher. I worked with her for a while, then when she left; I worked for the employee—still in language. Then an opening opened up as an Assistant in the Indian Child Welfare Department and I was hired by the Supervisor there in that office. The Supervisor was good enough to teach me everything that he knew and since he wanted to leave and go work in China as a missionary, he helped me get hired as the new Manager of Indian Child Welfare Act. The salary was good and I sincerely enjoyed working in that Department. I did not have any extra help so everything that needed to be done was done by me. I handled foster children in court situations whether it was tribal courts or Superior Courts throughout the United States. I traveled out of state a lot to courts there and became familiar with the system. I kept busy and know that I did an extremely good job for the people and the system. I took DNA tests to determine the parentage of the children. It was a good job, which really had little to do with the Yavapai-Apache Nation's court but with other tribes and the county; mostly in Arizona, California and Nevada.

Like I said, I liked the job; but when a new chairman got on board, he along with a nephew of mine, worked to get rid of me. There was a campaign of getting rid of "old" people from the workforce there at the Nation. The economy was going down and they figured one way to cut down expenses was to get rid of the "old people" of which, I was one! I had retired in Albuquerque before I moved to Clarkdale and so I had also been living on Social Security and working again. Dale and I were doing fine financially. Dale had quit his job at the Cement Plant and was at home helping me with other things. He even spent some time working for the Nation's Sand and Rock Board. The Lord blessed me with a young appearance so people always thought I was younger than I really was. I also was healthy as I like to exercise and go for daily walks. However, when they found about my age, they wanted me to quit working. I did not quit because I felt able and enjoyed working. At this point, a new person was hired as the Director of Social Services, a non-tribal member, who figured she knew everything and was constantly into my business. She spent more time in my office, cutting in on my cases and making determinations which I did not approve. My nephew, who was hired as the Business Manager for the Nation thought she was a terrific person and using her opinions of me, helped take my job from me. I had done nothing wrong and was torn up from losing that job. A whole year went by before I came around to trying to figure out what to do with myself. I felt that this was the end of the world for me—my life, my job and my future—everything looked hopeless! Time dragged on and I knew that I had to snap out of this phase and do something so I began work on my book.

I had on occasion began teaching the history of my tribe, "The Yavapai" at Yavapai College on a volunteer basis teaching several sessions when I felt like it so I then had that to keep me busy. The people loved my teaching and these people really didn't know much about Indians—especially the Yavapai since everyone knew more about the Apache. A lot of the people were mostly from out state, coming from back east, just living in Arizona for the summer months and they knew hardly anything about Indians. They were so good to me and built me up. I also taught the Yavapai Language for certain groups with the Nation, but most of the time, without compensation.

My granddaughter, Lexi wanted to work, but did not have her high school diploma so she attended GED classes and got her diploma -- then, she began working at the Casino. Always outgoing and friendly, she had several good jobs, but seemed to get in trouble always and mess up the job. She had grown into a beautiful girl; but this was just a disadvantage for her. She just seemed to attract the "wrong crowd" and would get herself into trouble. The first thing she got into, of course, was into drinking which she had started while still in New Mexico. Here in Arizona, she got into drugs also— mainly, meth. I didn't have a clue at first except that she told us at dinnertime one evening that she was going out but that she wanted us to know what meth did to the body and showed us her arm which had red bumps and also on her face. We were troubled but did not know what to do. She told me that even if I thought this little town was so great and far from the troubles in New Mexico that this place was worse and that it was so easy to get meth and that practically everyone used it here. Once, we called the tribal police about her drug use and they just talked to her and did not do anything. One night, she became paranoid and told us that there were motorcycles driving around in our yard. She was afraid to sleep alone and crawled into bed with Dale and me. She wrecked my little green Geo, which was paid for, and totaled it altogether. Lucky for her, she was not killed. Later, she wrecked a new sedan we bought for her, hitting the side of a hill. The car climbed a hill part way then turned and rolled backwards throwing her out of the car—almost landing on her. That car was totaled. Then, we got her another car which she managed to hit something and the front bumper was cracked and hanging. The Arizona Department of Motor Vehicles would not let her drive so we parked the car. We believed her when she said she would take the car to her boyfriend's house and just park it and we let her take it. However, she got caught driving it and since she was on probation, the police took her to jail. How we loved the girl and tried to get her things she wanted and always did what we could for her; but it backfired when she took advantage of the generosity we offered but really could not afford. She was just as much trouble as my sons had been with their drinking problems. Now, Lexi was gone and we missed her – there was just Dale and me.

Several years had gone by before my son Rico called and asked if he could come and live with us here in Arizona. He said that he and his wife were not getting along and that he had left his job with the Albuquerque Transit. He said he had nowhere to go. We told him to come live with us as we had the extra bedroom. However, when he came over, he started his drinking again and became the problem he was before.

Like others who drink I guess, he tends to get extra mean and argues and does not listen when he gets drunk. He got into so much trouble, getting stabbed by a Mexican illegal, getting a hairline fracture on his neck whereby he could have died. I believe that he does want to change, but does not have a wholehearted commitment to that effort. The woman that he says he loves now also has a history of drug use and alcohol. The couple fight constantly since being together. It is a real headache to me and something that I do not like having to deal with in my aging years. I have prayed and prayed over this problem and look forward to relief. The problem of alcohol addiction just seems to haunt me and has all my life!

My second son Wista was also an alcoholic and drug user and along with his diabetes problem he had to deal with a lot of health problems when getting out of jail and living by himself. It is sad that he never made a marriage work while with his girlfriends. He had one daughter and one son with women whom he never married and now has had to face his illnesses on his own.

This problem of alcoholism hits a lot of Native American families as it has hit mine. I had four of my sisters die of this alcohol problem and I know it is a terrible problem on the reservation even today. Also, today of course, is the problem with drugs (including prescription drugs) which the Native Americans also get into.

I have managed to survive that problem and I am so grateful to Almighty God for that! I believe and trust that my prayers were answered in that way and know that I do have a God that cares! However, I do not believe that it is an inherited problem with Native Americans as I am asked so many times by non-Natives. This alcohol problem is instead; a matter of "choice" as it is with everyone else (other races, and other nationalities).

I would like to go into my observation of the life of a Yavapai since coming back to the reservation and land of my ancestors. Tribal people would not accept me figuring that I was a "Newcomer" to the reservation and did not belong here. I have been criticized and looked down on by a lot of my own people. Although I am a fluent Yavapai Language speaker, I was not totally accepted as belonging here. If one person got angry with me or just didn't like the way I looked, I was hated by all of their relatives. Unfair as it was, it existed long ago and still does to this day. I have often thought of moving back to New Mexico where so many mixtures of people help eliminate situations like this. My husband Dale though, being the Christian that he is, always accepted bad situations and usually made things tolerable. Following his lead, I try to be more like him as it seems to work for him.

Working for the Nation as the Indian Child Welfare Manager, I dealt with a lot of problems affecting children of the Nation. It was so sad to see. I know that I did my best to see what I could do to alleviate the problems. One thing, I did gain was contact with people in regards to their stories about being,

Daniel Mendoza

The man that contacted me; with curiosity about his grandmother, and her plight as a child having been "Sold" into slavery and her memory of the Mining Camps at "Congress" and "Jerome".

Daniel and his family have become some of our closest friends.

Here I am between Linda and Daniel Mendoza; you can probably tell from the picture that they are a couple of "Ham Actors" to say the least.

Daniel and Linda Mendoza's Grandchildren: George Jr., Daniel, Theresa and Marissa Arroyo. ▶

Here we have a much earlier photo of Daniel Mendoza; his Daughter Reyna and Granddaughter Theresa Arroyo ▼ ▼

This whole family, which includes more members than we have pictures of here; are among our closest friends. In other words the whole Mendoza family is loved by; Dale and I.

"Indian Orphans". We know that way back in the history of the Nation and in the history of most of the Indian tribes, there was the capturing and the selling of Indian Children. Some descendants of those Indians who were captured and sold got in touch with me and relayed their stories. One such story is the story of Daniel Mendoza, a resident of San Diego, California. I have included his story, word for word so that others might know of the plight of Indians in those early days.

Ms. Frieda
As told by her grandson: Daniel Mendoza

As a kid we often heard that my grandmother was born April 05, 1903 in Arizona. From what I could remember is that my grandmother telling us kids that she remembers being in Jerome with red rocks all around and also living in Congress Junction, Arizona. We would sometimes ask my grandmother about her parents. She only remembered that her mother's name was Francesca. She told her family that her mother had died when she was a little girl. She never mentioned her father or what his name was, so we never asked her. She had no pictures and did not talk too much about her childhood but she did tell us a time about getting picked up for school in a wagon pulled by horses. She also mentioned as a little girl she remembered having scarlet fever.

We believe that my grandmother was raised in a Mexican family. We also believe that her name might have been changed to a Christian name, Frieda/Rita. After researching and talking to my grandmother's sister relatives, they told us that she was not blood related but adopted.

My grandmother had her first child, Sebastian, at the age of 16 in Calexico. Before the age of 16, we had no idea where she was at. There were no records kept of her having my uncle in Calexico. All we found was an affidavit of birth of my Uncle Sebastian, born 1919. The affidavit had my grandmother's name as Rita Freida.. I also located the birth certificate of my aunt Viola, born 1928 in the City of San Diego. The birth certificate had my grandmother's name as Rita Frada. The next time my grandmother was located, was in the April 7, 1930 census. We know that is 1930 she lived in Los Angeles. She lived there with her husband, Clarence Legerretta. She had four children at the time. The children's names were Sebastin, Rosie, Dolores and Viola. Shortly after she moved to San Diego and had her fifth child, my mother, Annie Legerretta,

July 22, 1930. The birth certificate had my grandmother's name as Rita Ferrieda. My grandmother's children didn't know too much about their mother's early life.

By the time I was born, all my grandmother's kids were grown and had started their families. My grandmother spoke English and Spanish. I believe because of being brought up speaking the other languages, my grandmother, her children, and her grandchildren lost their native culture, language and family history.

When I was around 8 years old, sometimes I would hear my aunts and my mother talking about my grandmother's drinking quite a bit and how they were all put in foster homes during April 1935. I was able to locate records from the San Diego Superior Court that awarded to place them in foster care. I remember asking my mother about grandma. She said that her mother was Yavapai from Arizona. As a kid I didn't know what Yavapai meant, so I just said, "Oh." I never knew that Yavapai was a tribe of Indians.

During the same time, my grandfather was not able to handle my grandmother's drinking so he ended up leaving her. About a year or two later, my grandmother met and married Jack

Aiken, who she stayed and lived with, until after his death. She had one child with Jack, named Jack Aiken, Jr. My grandmother worked at the West Gate Tuna Factory until the retirement age. I remember that she liked to knit and crochet and work in her garden. I also remember that she grew fruits and other plants. When the kids were sick instead of going to the doctor, she would gather some of her plants, smashed them up or boil them in water and would feed us a teaspoon of it. We would start to feel better after taking it.

As years went by, my grandmother developed Alzheimer's disease at around the age of 75. When we use to see her at my mother's house, she would watch western movies and get mad, she would often say that Indians don't act that way, they don't wear a bunch of feathers and don't make a bunch of loud noises. She said that they were the ones that they would shoot first. We asked her, grandma, what would they do? She would say, Indians were very quiet and they would sneak up on you. When she heard the Indian drum beats, she would rock and move her feet. We would look and ask her, "Grandma, why do you move your feet to the drum beats?" She would look at us and grin. My grandmother passed away on January 1, 1990 of Alzheimer's at the age of 86.

A few years after her death, our family became curious of my grandmother's history, of who she was and where she came from. So my cousins and relatives started searching for her history. They travelled to Arizona, San Carlos, Ft. McDowell and other reservations throughout Arizona looking for any record or traces. We visited my grandmother's sister's relatives, who were Mexican and they told us that my grandmother was not blood related to them but was raised by them. They told us that my grandmother never knew she was adopted by them. She believed that her sister, Kate, as her real sister. Unfortunately Kate passed away before my grandmother.

We also started asking my grandfather's relatives that were alive about my grandmother. They told us that my grandfather brought an Indian girl from Arizona and didn't know what tribe she came from but only knew that she was from Arizona. For the next ten years of research, until now, we will have not found any records or documents that would lead us to her family history. It's like she appeared and then disappeared with no trace. So we wanted to see what kind of DNA we had. So, me and most of my cousins took a DNA test and it showed that we all had over 50% of Native DNA. We asked the DNA technician what that meant. He said that we had an immediate family member that was Native American. He said if you had a great grandmother that was Native, your DNA would be somewhere around 12%. So we figured it was my grandmother that was native.

My grandmother has one child left who is alive, her name is Viola. She is 85 years old. About three years ago, I ran into her. I was wearing a cap that said, "Yavapai". When she saw it, she said that's where mama came from. I tried to ask her more about grandma, but like before she knew little about her mother's early years.

Now that many years have passed, there is no one left who has any information or knowledge about my grandmother. Even among all of my grandmother's grandchildren. We all basically know the same information about her. Some even know less. Unfortunately because we can't locate any records, we still continue to hit dead ends."

This then, is the story of my friend Daniel Mendoza and his family. For me it is so sad to know that nothing has been done to try to reunite Indians like this with their tribes. Their ancestors were taken and sold, lived another life with another group of people and now their descendants would like to know their own people. I, for one, feel the need to undertake this problem and do my best to help.

Sad as the Mendoza story is, here is another one that is even more so heartbreaking. It involves the story of a young Indian girl who was taken into a non-Indian household told in her own words. This is the story of a woman by the name of Judi West who believes that she comes from the Navajo Tribe. She is a brave woman but so hurt by the situation of not knowing for sure where she belongs.

"I am a Native American child, when I was 9 ½ months old, my birth mother sold me. At that time, it was acceptable to sell Native babies to white people. I remember being potty trained and if I messed up, my head was shoved in the toilet—back and forth. I fought hard not to touch the poop. I was so scared – I remembered trying so hard not to poop in my pants. It just seemed as if by the time I knew I had to go and tried to climbing the stairs to get to the bathroom, I just could not get up those stairs fast enough (I am two and half years old).

My father was in the military and we were in France the first two and half years of my life. I remember the flowers in the back and the dogs running around the gardens. I used to sit out there alone, petting the dogs. The dogs always

Each "Indian Orphan" has their own 'Identity Crisis', which is seldom even known; just a 'hollow spot': Some fair well; even with 'something' missing.

Cowgirl Friend from Tennessee "Judi West" and some of her friends; looks like a beautiful, peaceful place to be; but even there she has had some troubled times and has had "Growing Pains" of her own. No one has ever had Perfect: "Parents or Foster Parents"; "Grandparents that's different". ☺

Pretty as a picture aren't they? The horses seem to sense Judi's calm attentive "Beauty and Manner"; fantastic

were loving on me. Dog spelled backward is GOD, so I reflect back and see the comfort God sent me as a baby to comfort me.

I was three (3) years old (in California by this time) and I remember my mother picking me up by my feet and down I went on my head. I was crying and screaming. I heard her laugh and her deep breaths as she got out of breath from holding me upside down and slamming my head on the floor. My father did nothing to stop my mother—he watched. They made my brother watch too. I was small and scared with no one to protect me (feeling of helplessness). He was a big man, smart man served in two wars and she was a small woman- yet there was no comfort from my father. I remember looking at him wondering why doesn't he stop her.

I don't remember a day without a slap or a harsh word. "You're the Devil", "You're nothing": "You'll never amount to anything", "You act like a wild Indian", "You're a disgrace" or "You're retarded" there are more, -- but these seem to haunt me to this day. One day, my parents took me to the doctor and I had no idea why—these doctors were testing me in a room with sound, figures, and some kind of game. They took blood, x-rays and some kind of exam. Later they had me sit on a chair while they talked to my parents. I heard them tell them there is nothing wrong with your daughter. She is perfectly normal. My mother said, "There has to be something wrong with her—are you sure she isn't retarded?" As I sat there, I had no idea what retarded meant—I just knew it was bad, because that's what she would call me.

I remember going to school with bruises and welts on my legs. This too was acceptable at the time. No one said a thing. I could see other kids looking at me, but never said a thing. I guess they thought I was a really bad kid. I walked with my head always looking down at the ground. Ashamed of myself and not knowing why all I knew I wasn't like them and was not bad.

When I was seven years old, a friend of mine invited me to church -- to a Baptist Church. At first my mother would not hear of me going to a church; but she was asked every week and one Sunday to my surprise, my mother said I could go. Little did I know, but GOD had plans for me!

That Sunday was a day I will never forget. I walked into that church, and of course, everyone was white! I stood out, but everyone treated me nice. I heard and saw the kids smiling, laughing and running around and no one was telling them to hush or yelling at them.

I was a bit out of place, because everyone seemed happy (a feeling that I wasn't used to at all!). Then we went into a class room and there all the kids were busy -- and then, the teacher asked us all to sit while she would read a story to us. To this day, I don't remember the story. But, at the end of the story, the teacher turned to us (but I thought it was just me) and said, "Did you know that Jesus LOVES YOU!" I remember sitting in shock...because NO ONE had ever told me they loved me before—EVER! When I got home, I was so thrilled to know that Jesus LOVED ME! Yep, ME!

The parents that bought me did not treat me like their own child, but kind of like a step child or Cinderella, sort of, but worse. If I didn't clean the bathroom spotless and my mother came with her finger out and anything got on it, I was not only beaten, but had to redo it all again (powder ajax).

I was not allowed to go with the family (I was not included in family functions like family reunions.) I was always separated from everyone. They took me to a family funeral and made me sit alone—I must have been around eight years old at that time. My parents made me sit alone away from everyone else. I looked out at everyone and saw they all had someone to sit by them. I was seated where everyone could see me sitting all alone – yet no one came to sit with me. They just looked at me. I couldn't understand why I couldn't sit by my parents like the other kids.

Time went on—even after I got beatings, or harsh words, I'd just go into the closet in my room, close the door and talk to Jesus. I knew He loved me and I would cry to Jesus...talk to him—ask him why, oh why, does my mother do these things to me. Why doesn't she love me. I prayed to Jesus asking him to have her love me. I just wanted to be loved. I prayed and asked Jesus not to make me like her when I grew up. I prayed I would never be the mother she was to me to my own children. (At 8 years old, these were the type of prayers I would pray). I prayed and asked Jesus to not let me get hurt anymore. All the scriptures in the Bible about Jesus loves the little children, I held close to my heart. I read that he loved me. I re-read that Jesus Loved me just like the teacher said at Sunday School class.

As I got older, eight or nine years old, I stopped crying altogether. No matter how long the beatings were or how hard I was hit. No matter how bad even if or seen the blood dripped from my head. I didn't allow anyone anymore to see me cry. I wasn't going to allow anyone to think I was weak—especially my mother. Sometimes after a beating, I would go outside with the dogs and sit and pet them–asking Jesus to help me.

As I write this it hurts me deeply, because I truly believe in my heart now (I am much older) she loved me, but didn't know what she was doing. I feel she had a mental illness that affected her or she was mistreated as a child. So, please don't hate her. I love her no matter what. Just like Jesus loves me with all my faults, I love her too.

One day after my time in the closet and my talk with Jesus, I thought I am going to try and hug my mother that was on her heart. Maybe she will love me then. I walked down the hallway – I never been hugged before, so I got my courage up and walked where she was and opened my arms to hug her and she put her arm in a blocking motion and pushed me away. I stood there not knowing what to do.. I just froze—she walked away. I remember it hurt me so much like the worse than any beating I could imagine it hurt so bad! I can picture that moment to this day. I was such a little girl wanting to be loved. I wanted my mommie so bad.

The beatings were bad – she would beat me until she would get tired. There was blood dripping from my head where glass was broken over my head and my father came in and took me to the bathroom as he wiped my head and all the blood off. He didn't say anything. But to this one day, he took me for in the car for a ride and out of the silence, he said to me, "Your mother doesn't care for you because you didn't turn out the way that she thought you would." I remember looking out the window of the car taking it all in and wondering "how am I supposed to be." I never did say it though--just sat quietly.

When I was in the third grade, I had a teacher that was a Christian black woman. When I was nine, she took me in her arms and hugged me. She was big and mushed me in her arms—she held me tight. She turned out to be my third mother—a wonderful, loving Christian woman.

No matter what I did in life (and I could be a stinker at time) to my teacher; she never had a curse word or had a mean thing to say. She was like an angel.

I grew up in a pretty rough part of the world---I never liked it there. Jesus protected me even in the environment that I was raised. I was living in the ghetto (like East L.A. to describe it). I saw young people die. I remember a kid beaten in the gutter and I couldn't help. I remember going over there to try and help out but the guy that just beaten the other kid up pulled out a gun and pointed it at me and said, "If you don't go away, I will blow you away!" I looked and turned away because I was so terrified—the kid was already gone with all the blood that lay near his head. That image will never leave me. I prayed for his soul shortly after that. I was 14 or 15 at the time. Sill I felt so helpless that I couldn't help.

As a teenager, I was invited to some cool parties (I thought at the time I was cool). Major drug dealers would invite me to parties, but when someone would pass something (drugs) to me—they would tell the others, "No, don't give her anything, she is a good girl." I was stunned and didn't say anything. I heard this quite often wondering what they saw in me that I didn't see in myself. I never thought of myself as a good girl. (I never thought much of myself.) I didn't fit in with any group at high school (groups-gangs). Therefore, I tended to hand out mostly by myself. Yet, every head of a gang liked me and protected me. All I could think is that Jesus even made the bad people protect me. I didn't understand it at a young age.

Yes, I got into many fights growing up. The fights were very ugly. Yes, I hurt some and almost killed a couple. The feeling within me had no intention of hurting anyone ever. I didn't even want to fight, but where I lived, it didn't matter—it came the environment I lived in. It was like if you looked at someone wrong they wanted to fight. If you said "hi" to the wrong person, someone wanted to fight— senseless to me.

Even as a young person, before I would have to fight (there was no choice when someone wanted to fight you), I would pray to Jesus to protect me and not let them mess me up, because the fights were ugly.

I went to school and I worked full time too. I was pretty much on my own by 16 years old. I worked at a Convalescent Home doing the night shift. I lied about my age back then you didn't need proof of age. One night, I was jumped by two men —one with a Golden Sky Mask and the other with nylon stockings over their heads. I fought hard and bit down and finally the nurse and others came out running outside. The police came pretty fast and were amazed that I wasn't raped or worse. The lady that was supposed to go outside and get the linen fell asleep. She was 60 years old at that time. I thought she was really old to be working. I told the other girl that I would go out and get the linen. When I came back in the hospital, the lady hugged me and said, "I was supposed to have gone out there...." I told her, "They would have hurt you." The police agreed and told her the same thing, plus they said they had been watching the place because several of the lights outside were missing. God put me in a place and protected someone else. The police were so stunned by the description of the men (they were big). That all I had was a fat lip from biting so hard now on his hand when he went to cover my mouth. Jesus protected the lady, but gave me my life to help others. I didn't realize it at this point what that meant.

Growing older and trying to find out who I am. I know Jesus protected me no matter what happened in my life--no matter what difficulties I went through. Having a child out of wedlock back in the day when that was a cursed woman. Still, looking for love, but in the wrong places, I made many mistakes or I should say bad choices. Searching for love— little did I know I already had it with Jesus—it took me many, many years to realize it.

All the time while looking to be held and loved, searching endlessly, Jesus was always there protecting me and loving me—no matter what I did. No matter what color I am or what race I am. Jesus was always there. Today, I see he had a plan for me. Jesus was preparing my life for him and his purpose.

PINE RIDGE RESERVATION: Five years ago if someone would have said this is what I would be doing the place I would be visiting, I would have laughed in disbelief. On my first trip to the Pine ridge Reservation on the Crazy Horse Ride, "Honoring VET and Crazy Horse", I sat next to an elder at Pine Ridge Reservation. There he was looking up and I looked up and we were watching an eagle flying high in a circle. He quoted scripture: Isiah 40:31 but those who hope in the LORD will renew their strength. They will soar on wings like eagles; they will run and not grow weary, they will walk and not be faint.. And suddenly he turned to me and said, "You belong here." (Native Voice) and turned away—we continued to watching the eagle until we couldn't see it any longer. He had no idea. NO ONE in my life has ever said to me "I BELONGED." I almost lost myself. (crying inside)

I sat on a hill with a little native boy sitting by my side as I looked at all the kids playing and my heart was so blessed. God spoke to me and said, "This is where I want you and want you to unite my people." God also put on my heart that the 12 Tribes that are missing, "Natives are a Tribe."

With all my experiences in life, Jesus always carried me and he surrounded me with his Chosen People. He put the right people in my life to help me on my path. I know he was there watching over me and protecting me every step that I took to this day. One thing God never took my memories of what I went through as a baby and child. My heart still cries when I think of my childhood, but it gives me strength to help other children. I can still feel the pain and no child should carry this pain throughout their lives. I pray one day to reunite with my own people, "Navajo Nation" one day. As a child, have to deal with loneliness, fear, beatings, not loved, and worst of all, rejection. I pray one day that my walk here will make a difference to other children!

That was another of the "Orphan Indian" stories told to me—so sad and so heartbreaking! One was what I believed a Yavapai Orphan Story and the other, another tribe's orphan sold by her own mother. I made a vow to help these children and see what we can do for them. Of course, there are many other stories like these stories going way back when this country was first settled.

Looking back to when I was a young kid, I believed that Indians were the best people in the world and I was happy to be one of them. However, when I moved to the reservation in 2001 there was disappointment in store for me. My people (most of them) were still, for the most part, living, like it was still the 1800's saying things like, "The white people stole all our land!" When I hear this, I would always think to myself, that was a long, long, time ago and all white people aren't the same. You have to get to know people to understand them. I myself, have met a lot of whites in my time—some were bad and some were good—just like my great aunt, Maggie Hayes, said so long ago in those exact words, "white people are just like all other people—some are good and some are bad." I believe the same thing! My husband Dale is of German Ancestry and a very good Christian. He believes in "forgiveness" which I find is a hard thing to do when you have been hurt by someone. We, Dale and I, have a good relationship in our marriage and one that I hope lasts for now and for all eternity!

I am now up in my 70's and I know how blessed I am to have lived so long. I have eleven grandchildren, and four great-grandchildren that I am lucky to see and hold. I have endured hardships that I wouldn't wish on anyone else trying to raise my children when my first husband passed away at a young age. They say that life is not fair, and I know that is true -- it is can be very hard!

Only recently I have learned of the death of my second son who was living in Albuquerque. He used to call me every day morning and night until one day he didn't call. Not hearing from him, I called his pastor to check on him. The pastor sent someone to check on him and they found my son had his door open and was lying there on his bed. He had passed away and so they notified the pastor who called us. We, the family, drove to Albuquerque the next day. We did not find his wallet, money or his cell phone— someone went into his room and took these things. The mortuary did not check for trauma as his visual signs looked all right and his history of illness made them believe that nothing was wrong—so they put down his death as a heart attack. I don't know what really happened nor will I ever know the truth and my heart aches for my son and what he might have gone through in his final hours! I will miss his calls and his chats with me about sports. I love sports— football, baseball, basketball everything; and he would keep me informed. He knew I went to the University of Kansas so he got a KU cap and always wore it telling people, "My mom went to school there!" He was so proud of me. I will miss him! I only know that whoever took his belongings as he laid there already departed will one day have to answer to the Lord.

SUMMARY

Since returning to my reservation, I can say that I found it to be a very difficult experience from what I knew growing up off of the reservation. There was prejudice and name calling, hatred for Indians but I endured those off of the reservation. Here, on my reservation, I can see that living here also brings its own problems. When are things going to change for the better? As I said, living on the outside, growing up off of the reservation, I didn't really know the problems on the reservation. Since moving here and living here I can see the problems that have developed because of assimilation into the white society. There are still the words, "I'm just an Indian." Alcohol and drugs still play a big part for the Indians who are still feeling the pains (real or unreal) of being a defeated group of people with no hope for progress. The Indian blood lines are thinning out and soon there will be no more full-blood Indians.

So, this book summarizes the lives of my ancestors, siblings and descendants. I have gone through very tough times losing my husband early on and losing two sons; and I have struggled with some of my children and their addiction problems; but now they are beginning to realize the importance of striving ahead. I continue living my life, always trying to do my best to withstand bad times after all, I am Yavapai and we, the Yavapai, are survivors; and with an Almighty God who stands by our side, we (the Yavapai) will continue to survive!

I know that the reflections of my father, "Samuel Adams Russell", my grandmother, "Jun Tha La Charley", and my great Aunt "Maggie Hayes", are all what make this a somewhat unique account of family and reservation life. Since moving back to the reservation in my late years these are my personal thoughts! "Reservation Life", as a whole, is to a large degree the Socialistic base of Governance which does a lot to stifle the "Creativity" and "Ingenuity" of American Indians as a whole. In other words, I believe that the Bureau of Indian Affairs is attempting to hold the American Indians under the government's thumb, in order to, "Justify the Need" for the continued existence of a continued Bureaucracy which makes or holds the people as a "Dependent Class". Dr. Carlos Montezuma, of long ago, and other thoughtful people including military personnel from that time period in the early 1900's, expressed very similar opinions. The hypocrisy of the difference between what well meaning "Denominational Christians" presented and the words and actions of the settlers, railroad workers, cowboys and soldiers; bred confusion and disdain, for the "Whiteman" and with "Broken Promises and Treaties" that seemingly came with, every change of wind, "Indian Agent" or "Military Leader". The "Will to Achieve has been rapidly lost and the make-believe "so-called Government Benevolence" does nothing to replace the need for "Pride of

Accomplishment". I was fortunate in the fact that my father and grandmother instilled into my upbringing a need for a good "Work Ethic and Self-Reliance", without which, I would probably would have let go of my knowledge of the past and my Christian upbringing in favor of the instant gratification of mediocrity that I have seen on the other side.

With the rest of my life, I am going to do my best in Preserving my Native Yavapai Language and History; even though I believe that my efforts should at least be recognized by the Yavapai and Apache Tribal Nation, to which I am a lifelong member. My satisfaction in this project comes in part from the recognition, some from the hope of some financial success and, most of all, from the belief that somehow I will leave this world a mite better for having been here~

NUV LITHE (THAT IS ALL)

In back all six are named "Eswonia": On this side; L2R Marie, Leroy III, Emily and I'm holding, My Great Granddaughter; Marie's baby.

In back on this side: L2R Center; Alexia, Eugene and Julie. Seated beside me is Dale; he should have been happy ; he did not even have to pay the bill.

My Family; My Birthday Party 2014 some of my grandchildren, I am holding my Great Grandchild Layla and Dale looks Grumpy even without his; "Grumpy's Garage Shirt and Cap"

Hawaiian Cruise

Dale and I; Ashore on a Hawaiian Cruise that was fantastic. One of the highlights of the cruise was when we were at a Native Hawaiian Village and Dale and I "Renewed Our Wedding Vows"; and we were entertained by the local Tribe singing, dancing, and laughing as they shared a great traditional meal with us.

The awesome beauty of the Islands and the Island People is spectacular and our trip was an outstanding experience that we will never forget; and would dearly love to repeat if we ever have the chance.

Hawaiian Cruise

Being treated as dignitaries; with the Cruise Ship's Capitan.

Happy Looking Couple

My Granddaughter Alexia Eswonia with her boyfriend Chad oh, ah, ah, "whatshisname"

And over here to the right we see Alexia and Chad's Cat getting some 'Rest'; whether it is deserved rest or not I'm just not at all sure.

My only daughter "Sherrilee" called "Doe" she is my baby, the family stabilizer, and quick-witted comic; she is special.

Made in the USA
Middletown, DE
14 February 2019